YES, YOU CAN TRAVEL WITH KIDS

A **NO-STRESS GUIDE** *to* **EASY, AFFORDABLE FAMILY TRAVEL**

YES, YOU CAN TRAVEL with KIDS

JENNA CARR

First published in Great Britain in 2026 by
DK RED, an imprint of
Dorling Kindersley Limited
20 Vauxhall Bridge Road,
London SW1V 2SA

The authorised representative in the EEA is
Dorling Kindersley Verlag GmbH. Arnulfstr. 124,
80636 Munich, Germany

Copyright © 2026 Dorling Kindersley Limited
A Penguin Random House Company
10 9 8 7 6 5 4 3 2 1
001–352113–Feb/2026

Text copyright © 2026 Jenna Carr

Jenna Carr has asserted her right to
be identified as the author of this work.

Page 10: Steve Jobs, Stanford Commencement Address,
Stanford University, CA, June 12, 2005.

Cover design and illustration by Mary Kate McDevitt

All rights reserved.
No part of this publication may be reproduced, stored in or introduced into
a retrieval system, or transmitted, in any form, or by any means (electronic,
mechanical, photocopying, recording, or otherwise), without the prior
written permission of the copyright owner.

DK values and supports copyright. Thank you for respecting intellectual
property laws by not reproducing, scanning or distributing any part of this
publication by any means without permission. By purchasing an authorised
edition, you are supporting writers and artists and enabling DK to continue
to publish books that inform and inspire readers.

No part of this publication may be used or reproduced in
any manner for the purpose of training artificial intelligence technologies or
systems. In accordance with Article 4(3) of the DSM Directive 2019/790,
DK expressly reserves this work from the text and data mining exception.

A CIP catalogue record for this book
is available from the British Library.
ISBN: 978-0-2417-6785-6

Printed and bound in the United Kingdom

www.dk.com

To my boys Leo and Luca – may you always stay curious and ready for adventure.

CONTENTS

Introduction   8

PART ONE:
PENNY-PINCHING PLANNING   12

Chapter 1
Setting a Realistic Budget (And Sticking to It!)   18

Chapter 2
Flights and Transport   36

Chapter 3
Beds on a Budget   56

My Planning Checklist   76

PART TWO:
DESTINATION DECISIONS   78

Chapter 4
Deal Destinations   88

Chapter 5
The Art of the Family Road Trip
(Without Losing Your Sanity)   106

Chapter 6
Staycation Savvy   122

Chapter 7
Clever Camping — **140**

My Top 10 Sustainable Travel Tips — **164**

**PART THREE:
GROWING TOGETHER** — **166**

Chapter 8
Bumps, Bags and Babymoons — **174**

Chapter 9
Travelling with a Baby — **190**

Chapter 10
Travelling with Little Kids — **208**

Chapter 11
Travelling with Big Kids — **224**

My Most-Asked Questions — **246**

**Final Thoughts:
Just Start** — **248**

With Thanks — **250**
Index — **252**

INTRODUCTION

There I was, 32 weeks pregnant, scrolling through my Instagram feed full of sun-soaked beaches and bikini-clad beauts sipping on cocktails by infinity pools.

Why would they post that photo and not tell us where it is? I thought to myself as I rolled my eyes and reached for my seventh chocolate digestive (but who's counting?). Why is it always young, single women travelling the world and living their best lives? Where are all the parents? My 30th birthday was looming and it felt like the end of an era. I looked down at my big pregnant belly and thought, *Well, I guess this is it; maybe our travel days are over.*

I'd spent my twenties working as an NHS doctor and travelling the world in between. Travel had always felt like more than just a holiday for me – like it was my calling. I knew I had to do it, I knew it was important, but I struggled to articulate exactly why.

In 2017, a lucky swipe on Tinder landed me in a situation I wasn't expecting – I fell in love with a beautiful Portuguese man called João while travelling alone in the Algarve. Now, worse things *have* happened, but it was the last thing on my 2017 bingo card. What followed was a whirlwind romance measured in Ryanair flight receipts and weekend trips between my hometown of Sheffield and the Algarve.

Eighteen months later and there I was – elephant cankles, demolishing a pack of chocolate digestives and rolling my eyes at strangers living their best lives on social media.

Like many mums-to-be, I was staring down the barrel of maternity leave with statutory maternity pay that would barely cover my biscuit requirements. Working as a locum doctor had been great for funding my travel addiction, but without a permanent contract I wasn't eligible for full maternity pay. My Portuguese lover had swapped his engineering career in the sunny Algarve for dark and dreary Sheffield, and – as we quickly discovered – getting work as a foreigner wasn't as easy as we'd hoped. I'd been living in my parents' attic between adventures, and now João had joined me up there while we figured out a plan.

I'd always had a perfectly sensible life plan – or at least, that's what I told people: get a "proper" job with a pension, work solidly for a few years, build some savings, *then* think about starting a family. You know, the responsible way of doing life.

But as most of us learn sooner or later, life rarely goes to plan.

Never in a million years would I have imagined myself heavily pregnant, on the brink of 30, living in my parents' attic and sharing takeaways with a man I'd met on Portuguese Tinder not so long ago. On paper, it read like a Netflix rom-com written after one too many Vinho Verdes. But in reality? It felt right.

I've learned that when something huge and unexpected like this happens, you have to trust that things are happening for a reason. It has always rung true for me. Steve Jobs once said, "[it's] impossible to connect the dots looking forward, you can only connect them looking backward," and it was very true in this stage of my life.

As people started giving me those knowing smiles and patronising nods, dropping pearls of wisdom like, "Ah, you'll have to finally *settle down* now that you're pregnant" or "Say goodbye to all those holidays, hun," something inside me would snap. Maybe it was the pregnancy hormones. Maybe it was the fact that I'd just had to ask my mum to lend me and my baby daddy a fiver for a kebab. Or maybe, just maybe, I was scared they might actually be right. But I just knew we would have to make it work. I was determined that we would work out how to travel as a family, but on a very tight budget.

And so, with a biscuit in one hand and my ever-growing bump in the other, the next chapter of our lives began … This wasn't the end of my travel story; it was actually the beginning of a whole new adventure.

WHY I WROTE THIS BOOK

If you're reading this, maybe you're a new parent, wondering whether travel is still possible now that your life has changed. Or maybe you're pregnant, scrolling through glamorous holiday snaps on social media and wondering where you now fit in. I see you – because I *was* you.

This book was born from that moment of doubt – sitting in my parents' attic, very pregnant, very broke, and feeling like the adventurous life I'd loved was over. But what followed was proof that a new kind of adventure was only just beginning. And not only was it possible to keep travelling as a family, but, with a bit of creativity, a lot of determination and some serious budgeting, it could even be better than before.

We're now a family of four: me, my husband João, my eldest son Leo and my youngest son Luca. I wrote this book to show you how we make it work – and how you can too. Whether you're navigating airports with a baby, planning a summer holiday on a shoestring or trying to find the courage to take that first trip, this book is full of practical tips and encouragement to help you feel confident about family travel. Along the way, I've woven in my own story – not for drama, but to show how life can take you from one extreme to another. I share it all because I want you to see that life changes. Things fall apart and come back together in unexpected ways. Experiences shape us. And no matter where you are right now, more is possible than you think.

You don't need to be rich, or brave, or perfect – just willing to try. I'll take you through everything I've learned, from booking bargain flights to packing for toddler meltdowns at 30,000 feet, and then all the chaos in between. This isn't about flawless Instagram holidays; it's about real, messy, joyful adventures with the people you love.

Let's prove them wrong – our travel days are *not* over.

Part One
PENNY-PINCHING PLANNING

I was in my third year of working as a doctor when I discovered wilderness and expedition medicine. That is, working as a doctor in remote locations that don't have easy access to regular healthcare. This new potential career came about in an unusual way. In 2015, I applied for, and unexpectedly got accepted onto, a reality TV show. The concept seemed simple: I'd live in the Scottish wilderness with a bunch of other maniacs and provide medical care if anyone needed it. Combining medicine with an adventure? Right up my street. It turned out to be an experience that completely changed the direction of my life, one that taught me to appreciate the little things, and how the best things in life actually don't cost very much.

The basic plan for this TV show was that 21 strangers, each with a supposedly vital skill, would come together to build a self-sufficient community. A back-to-basics social experiment. Think *Survivor* meets *The Hunger Games*, just with more chickens and slightly less violence. We were fenced into a remote stretch of Scottish wilderness and left to figure it all out – no phones, no internet, no contact with the outside world. Ethics approval? I doubt it would stand a chance today.

We built shelters by chopping down trees, grew what food we could, fished, farmed animals and – the hardest bit by far – tried to get along with each other. It was raw, intense and an incredibly unique experience that changed my entire outlook on life. Shivering on the frozen ground, wearing every scrap of clothing I owned, surrounded by snow and sheltered only by a makeshift roof of hay and tarpaulin, it really put life into perspective. We didn't have a toilet or toilet paper – we had a hole in the ground and some dry moss to wipe with if we were lucky. Without a shower our only way to wash was in an ice cold stream or in the sea. Everyday essentials that we all take for granted were stripped away.

For months, we lived off potatoes. Even when the crops began to grow, you needed a lot of produce to feed 21 people; there just wasn't enough. Imagine hosting a dinner party for 21 people but having only potatoes ... That was our reality, all day, every day. We spent our days doing hard, physical labour: chopping wood, hauling water, building shelters. Then we'd collapse onto the freezing, hard floor at night, trying to sleep through the hunger and the cold.

And this wasn't a few days of discomfort. This went on for months.

The excess we take for granted in everyday life became glaringly obvious. Inside that camp, a small 'luxury' item held the power of gold. I remember someone giving a £200 IOU in exchange for a Chupa Chups lolly. We would use teabags endless times. I once found a scrap of potato peel in the sand and roasted it over the fire to make a crisp – we were that hungry. Anything slightly indulgent – a splash of hot sauce, a stick of chewing gum – became priceless.

It taught me a lot about resilience, gratitude and just how warped our sense of "need" becomes when we live in so much comfort. At times, it felt like torture: the constant cold, the gnawing hunger, the sheer exhaustion from physical labour and emotional strain. But alongside the suffering, there was something strangely beautiful. Stripped of all the noise and clutter of modern life, we started to notice joy in the smallest things.

We had nothing, and yet some nights we would lie on the cold ground, staring up at the stars surrounded by people who had gone from strangers to family – laughing until our bellies hurt despite having almost nothing in them. A single lollipop, passed between friends, brought the kind of joy you don't really get to experience in normal life. Try telling someone back home that a group of people shared one strawberry lolly and it was the highlight of the week and they'd look at you like you'd gone mad. But that's the thing about living with less: it strips away the nonsense. It sharpens your senses. You suddenly notice what actually matters – connection, humour, grit, the ability to find something to smile about even on the days when your socks are wet, your bum is mossy and your dignity has long gone.

It also completely rewired how I think about money and material items. That experience is why I plan the way I do — why I care about value over flash, and why this part of the book is about practical, penny-smart choices that buy you freedom and memories, not stuff.

… Chapter One
SETTING A REALISTIC BUDGET (AND STICKING TO IT!)

I remember the first time I searched for flights for our family and questioned why family travel was always portrayed as an unaffordable luxury. Since my experience in the Scottish wilderness, luxury was never something I strived for, or even wanted. Expensive package holidays just didn't appeal to me. I knew that cheaper trips meant more trips, and that is what I needed. I would look for the cheapest flights, find affordable accommodation and build my own "DIY trips".

For our first family trip, I had found £25 return flights to Gran Canaria, making the flights under £100 for the three of us: me, João and our son Leo. Budget airlines usually don't include any luggage, but what a lot of people don't realise is that you are allowed to take an under-seat bag for free. By packing light into three under-seat rucksacks, we would save a lot of money. Babies also have a check-in allowance for their pram / car seat, and this is usually included in the basic price. Once I had found the flights, I tracked down an apartment that was £200 for the week. Flights and accommodation for our family for under £300? For a whole week? Absolute bargain. And while that was, in fact, a steal, I was about to learn that flights and accommodation are merely the tip of the iceberg.

This is when I started to realise that finding the best-value holiday isn't always as simple as booking everything separately and creating your own DIY trip. While DIY travel can work out cheaper, it isn't a guarantee – especially when you factor in the extra layers that come with a family trip. I'm often asked, "Is all-inclusive cheaper than self-catering?" and my honest answer is, "Sometimes." Or, "Is it cheaper to book an apartment instead of a hotel?" Again, "Sometimes." What works out cheaper for me might not be cheaper for you. The cost of a holiday depends on how you like to travel, where you're going, how big your family is, whether anyone has additional needs, if you drink alcohol, whether you have any dietary requirements ... and much more.

In this chapter, we'll explore all the factors you'll need to think about when planning and budgeting for your trip, so you can work out what's best for you.

HIDDEN COSTS

Let's talk about what a holiday really costs – because that tempting £199 deal rarely tells the full story. I've learned the hard way that budgets often need to stretch far beyond what you initially expect, and some expenses are more "hidden" than others.

Take accommodation, for example. That bargain hotel you found? It might not seem so cheap when you arrive and discover a mandatory tourist tax that is charged per person, per night. Always check the small print so you're not caught off guard. A hotel may look the cheapest, but if the others include the tourist tax and the cheaper option doesn't, you haven't made the saving you had hoped for. Extra charges for essentials like a cot have also surprised us more than once. You knew we were bringing a baby, but now we have to pay for the privilege of him having a bed? Absolutely wild (but keeping it real, he never sleeps in it anyway; his preferred spot is sprawled across my face).

We really like booking small, family-owned accommodation or rentals. When you book directly with property owners, they often go the extra mile to make your stay special, without adding on extra fees for everything. We once asked for a high chair, and an hour later the owner turned up with a brand-new one from the supermarket!

Food

Food is one of the best parts of travel – the excitement of menus in a language you barely understand, the thrill of ordering your favourite meal made in its country of origin, spaghetti carbonara but made in a cute little restaurant in Italy? Yes please. And when you're converting euros to pounds after your third Aperol spritz, suddenly everything seems well-priced. Eating out and enjoying the local cuisine is one of my favourite parts of travelling, but eating in restaurants three times a day will obliterate your budget in no time.

Estimating food expenses can be tricky, though self-catering is a great way to save money, even if you don't self-cater for every meal. There's nothing better than fresh croissants and hot coffee on your balcony, and it'll cost a fraction of a proper café breakfast. Kids, too, are usually much happier munching on cereal in their PJs than sitting in a café where they have to behave. If you've ever tried keeping a toddler still in a restaurant, you'll also know that cooking up some simple pasta for dinner while they roam free in your apartment isn't just budget-friendly – it's a sanity-saver.

Supermarkets are the best option for feeding a family on a tight budget – I always track them down before visiting a place. We often make meals for under £10 and stocking up on supermarket snacks will also save you a small fortune when the kids start asking for ice creams five times a day. More importantly, a few bottles of wine from the shop? A fraction of the price of those at a restaurant. I have some recipe ideas for low-cost family meals (that can be cooked on a tiny two-ring hob, *p74*). But let's be honest – we can't scrimp on everything. A holiday wouldn't be a holiday without a long, leisurely dinner with a sunset view. It's all about finding a balance. We usually pick one or two special meals to splurge on and keep everything else simple. Eating where the locals eat gives a far more authentic experience and keeps costs down. Eating out at lunch, when menus are often cheaper, instead of dinner can also save a lot of money. A 9pm dinner with overtired kids rarely creates fun, cherished memories.

If you're considering staying in a hotel and it offers different meal plans (such as self-catering, half-board or all-inclusive), compare the price difference between each and note it down as "food costs". This will help you decide whether upgrading to a meal plan is worth it or if mixing self-catering and dining out will be more cost-effective. We recently stayed in a hotel where it was cheaper to book with breakfast

FINDING WHERE THE LOCALS EAT

Eating where the locals eat not only saves you money, it gives you a better, more authentic taste of the destination.

- **Step away from the main attractions:** Sounds obvious, but the closer you are to a landmark, the higher the prices will likely be. Wander a few streets back for better value and more authentic food.
- **Check where's busy with local people:** If it's full of people speaking the local language, or you see a long line waiting to get in, you're on to a winner.
- **Avoid the places where staff are trying to pull you in:** If you're like me, there is nothing worse than walking down a street and being stopped every five metres by someone trying to convince you to come inside to eat. This is a sure sign it is aimed at tourists.
- **Look at the menu:** If it's available in five languages with pictures, it's probably aimed at tourists. A simple, handwritten menu is usually a really good sign!
- **Use apps like Google Maps or TripAdvisor cleverly:** Search for places rated highly by locals, not just tourists. Look out for reviews in the native language too.
- **Ask your host, taxi driver or even a shopkeeper:** Locals are usually proud of their favourite spots and are happy to share them. Specifically, say you want to avoid the tourist spots.

included over the room-only rate. It makes no sense, but we booked and we didn't complain.

To estimate the cost of eating out, you can check restaurant menus online. Many places list their prices on their websites. I'm not suggesting you try to calculate the exact bill, but knowing whether a beer costs £3 or £15 will give you a good idea of what you're in for. I like to use apps like Google Street View to explore the area, looking for smaller cafés or street food vendors that might offer a quick, budget-friendly meal.

Once you have a rough daily food budget, multiply it by the number of days you'll be away. Always overestimate, because the kids spotting an ice cream stand (or Mum finding a two-for-one cocktail deal) is practically inevitable. Later in the book, we'll go into food-inclusive packages and when they might be worth it *(p62)*, but, ultimately, the budget you set for food depends on the type of trip you want. It really can be as little or as extravagant as you want it to be.

Transportation

You book some cheap flights and feel smug about your bargain-hunting skills, only to land and realise the airport is roughly the same distance from your hotel as home. Flying to Paris-Beauvais Airport? You're a whole hour and 20 minutes away from the city centre. And while you might find some incredible deals to Frankfurt Hahn Airport, you'll be surprised to discover you're not actually flying to Frankfurt – the airport is 120km (75 miles) from Frankfurt itself. This is how you can easily end up paying more for a taxi than you did for the flight!

I've learned (often the hard way) that researching public transport options beforehand is an absolute must. Buses, trains and metro passes can save you a fortune. Thankfully, you won't be the first person to land at the airport needing to reach a popular tourist destination. Chances are, there's already an established public transport route in place. With no prior research, though, it is easy to turn up and feel overwhelmed by a foreign public transport system, and ultimately opt for an expensive taxi. When planning your transport budget, consider every leg of your journey as it all adds up:

- How will you get from your home to the airport?
- What's your plan for getting from the airport to your hotel?
- How will you travel from your hotel to beaches and attractions?

If everything's within walking distance – bonus! Or perhaps there's a free hotel shuttle service? If you're considering renting a car *(p111)*, factor in the hidden costs: petrol, insurance and cleaning fees (because sand and sunscreen get EVERYWHERE, and children have no chill).

Activities and attractions

Attractions can also be a real budget-buster if you're not careful. Those entry fees add up fast – before you know it, you've spent the equivalent of a month's rent on a couple of zoo tickets and a boat tour.

> **TOP TIP**
> **Research attraction prices before your trip and plan accordingly.**
> Trust me on this one – once the kids spot something they want to do, you won't hear the end of it. It's much easier to have a game plan ready and suggest pre-researched options to them, before they set their hearts on something that would blow your budget.

Theme parks and water parks deserve special consideration (and have a section later in the book – *p134*). Always, ALWAYS check the height restrictions before booking anything. There's nothing worse than paying full price for a bunch of tickets, only to discover your little one can only go on two rides. (Cue the tears – and not just from the kids. I remember crying at the end of a long day when Leo couldn't get into the LEGOLAND® driving school!)

Here's how we make our holiday budget stretch further when it comes to activities:

- **Hit the local beaches, parks and hiking trails:** Set challenges for small kids, like who can find the best stone or leaf. Older kids may enjoy hiring a kayak or bike.
- **Do a free walking tour:** Make it fun for small kids with your own bingo card (spot a fountain, a dog in a jumper, a statue, and so

on). Get your bigger kids to help navigate with Google Maps and find highlights along the way.
- **Explore playgrounds:** These are great for your kids to socialise with local children!
- **Visit free museums:** Many museums in Europe have free admission on the first Sunday of the month. At the time of writing, the Louvre in Paris is free on the first Friday of the month in the evening. Make sure you look for options at your destination. Be aware that they will be much busier at these times.
- **Go later in the day:** Lots of attractions – zoos, aquariums, water parks – offer discounts if you go later in the day. You can usually pay a lot less for the final couple of hours. Often short and sweet is exactly what you need with kids.
- **Spend lazy days by the pool or utilise the kids' club if your hotel has one:** A win for all ages.
- **Visit nearby hotels:** Even if you are in a basic hotel, nearby resorts will likely allow outsiders to buy an evening drink at the bar. Translation: £3 Coke for the kids = free kids' disco, magician or bingo night. Entertainment sorted without paying resort prices.
- **Wander through local markets:** Perfect for soaking up the culture and eating lots.
- **Try the local library:** Many libraries abroad have free kids' activities or play corners. These are the perfect rainy-day saviour and they're often air-conditioned (double win).

If there's a must-see attraction on your list, always check for online booking discounts. Spoiler alert: booking ahead almost always saves you money. Many attractions will have special family packages – these are always worth investigating during the planning stages.

Miscellaneous

Just when you think you've accounted for everything, the sneaky extras appear: travel insurance, roaming charges, tips (tipping culture varies wildly depending on where you go) and the irresistible souvenirs that always seem to multiply in your suitcase (fridge magnets are an essential for us!). The key to all of this? Planning. Boring, I know, but how else will you stop things spiralling out of control? (Use the budget planner at the end of this section to help, *p34*.)

Travel insurance

Travel insurance is not just another optional extra – it's as essential as your passport. Whether you're booking a package holiday or going DIY, proper coverage is non-negotiable (unless you fancy remortgaging your house to cover unexpected hospital bills!).

> **TOP TIP**
> **An annual policy will likely be the best option for multiple trips.**
> Our annual family coverage was only around £85 at the time of writing – bargain! Always compare prices using comparison sites to snag the best deal. Many premium bank accounts or workplace benefit schemes may quietly include travel insurance, so always check. An annual policy is often cheaper and means less admin.

What to look for in your policy:
- **Medical coverage:** This is the biggie! Medical emergencies abroad can legit cost more than your house.
- **Luggage coverage:** Be realistic – if your entire holiday wardrobe costs less than £1,000, you don't need £3,000 of coverage. "Gadget cover" for devices is usually an optional extra.
- **Excess amounts:** Can you afford the excess if you need to claim?
- **Activity coverage:** Planning on skiing, scuba diving or anything adventurous? Make sure it's included!
- **Cruise cover:** Standard annual policies rarely include cruises. If you're planning to set sail, bolt on cruise cover separately.

Roaming charges

These catch a lot of people out. Before you travel, check whether your mobile provider includes roaming in your destination. If it doesn't, you have two options:

The simple solution – perfect for occasional internet checks:
- Switch off mobile data roaming.
- Stick to Wi-Fi when available. Most hotels, cafés and restaurants will have it.
- Download offline maps. This saves the "We're lost in the middle of Rome with two screaming kids and no signal" drama.

The eSIM solution – a great way to control your costs upfront:
- Choose a provider, then purchase an eSIM (downloaded via an app) for your destination.
- You get to keep your phone number.
- Choose between unlimited data or prepaid packages.

If one parent buys a big eSIM package, they can hotspot to everyone else. That way, you don't need four separate SIMs bleeding your budget. If you're travelling with older kids, put parental controls on their data use. Otherwise, they'll chew through your package on TikTok before you've even left Arrivals. Some eSIMs work across multiple countries – perfect if you're country-hopping. Just check the coverage areas before you buy.

HOW YOU SPEND

How you spend is just as important as *what* you spend. This was something I overlooked for a long time. I remember returning from one of our early trips and spotting £75 in transaction fees on my account. It turned out the card I had been tapping away with was charging me £1 every single time I used it! Many bank accounts apply transaction fees abroad and, while contactless payments are convenient, especially when your hands are full, it's really important to only use a travel-specific card that won't charge you. There are plenty of great options available, and using one can save you a significant amount of money over time.

On a similar note, be mindful of exchange rates and ATM charges. We use a variety of travel credit cards that offer near-perfect exchange rates when spending abroad. It's worth looking into these, as well as prepaid travel cards. A prepaid card can help you stick to a budget by allowing you to load a set amount of spending money onto it, making it easy to see when those extra mojitos start nudging your budget off course!

ATM fees also vary widely. As a general rule, avoid ATMs in hotels and airports, as they tend to have extortionate fees. Instead, look for ATMs attached to local banks. On a recent trip, the ATM in our hotel charged £8 just to withdraw cash, while the one across the road, which was linked to a bank, only charged £1.50. To minimise withdrawal fees, take out a larger sum of money rather than making multiple small withdrawals.

> **TOP TIP**
> **Always pay in the local currency when given the option.**
> Selecting your home currency may seem convenient, but it often comes with poor exchange rates and hidden fees.

FAMILY-SPECIFIC CONSIDERATIONS

As your family grows, you will start to realise just how much family size – and family dynamics – impacts every aspect of travel. For families of three, things are relatively simple – most standard hotel rooms accommodate two adults and a child, often with a sofa bed or option to bed-share. Families of four can still find plenty of hotel options, though it can be a little trickier. The real challenge comes for families of five or more, because many standard hotel rooms won't accommodate over four guests. With package holidays, larger families are frequently allocated two separate hotel rooms. This significantly increases the cost and is impractical, especially with small kids.

If you all want to be in the same space, booking everything yourself (DIY) can be a much more budget-friendly option. Opting for larger apartments or villas not only keeps everyone together, but also provides more space and privacy compared to multiple hotel rooms. We'll look at all-inclusive versus self-catering accommodation in more detail in Chapter Three. Beyond family size, other factors can impact travel plans:

- **Families with mobility issues:** Check accessibility carefully, as many older hotels and budget stays lack lifts or step-free access. Apartment rentals provide more flexibility, and some resorts have wheelchair-friendly rooms, but they are limited and book up fast.
- **Single parents:** Look out for companies that cater specifically to solo parents to avoid paying over the odds. Lots of companies offer solo traveller discounts to help make things more affordable. Choosing family-friendly accommodation with kids' clubs can also make a huge difference by occupying the kids for free, and giving you a bit of "me time".
- **LGBTQ+ families:** You should feel safe and welcome wherever you travel, but, unfortunately, that's not always the case. Researching local laws and attitudes is important, and staying in well-reviewed, inclusive accommodations can make the experience much more comfortable.
- **Neurodiverse families:** You may want to prioritise quieter accommodation options, flexible mealtimes and sensory-friendly attractions. Self-catering stays can help manage food preferences and routines, and some destinations now offer autism-friendly programmes with fast-track access and quiet spaces. *(See also "Neurodiverse Families: What to Know", p54.)*

Every family's needs are different, so a little extra planning can go a long way in making sure everyone has a stress-free (or at least, lower-stress) holiday!

MAKING YOUR DREAM TRIP A REALITY

When it comes to saving for your dream family trip, there are some simple ways to make things a little easier ...

Set realistic timelines

This is key. Start by estimating the total cost (use the budget planner at the end of this section to make notes, *p34*) and work backwards.

THE WHOOPS FUND

We factor this into every trip and, without fail, we end up needing it. I'd love to think most families are less chaotic than ours, but kids and exhaustion do strange things to a person. We try to budget around £200 for the Whoops Fund, hoping we won't actually need it.

A few recent examples of where the Whoops Fund has saved the day include:

- Our plane was delayed, which meant we missed the last bus and had to fork out for an expensive taxi. Whoops Fund.
- We once carried a sleeping child into the car, forgetting to put his shoes on (or pack any), and only realised on parking the car at the airport that he was about to spend the holiday barefoot. (Mum brain is wild.) Whoops Fund.
- We've also forgotten swim shorts +/– goggles more times than I care to admit ... Whoops Fund.
- We forgot to check in online for a Ryanair flight and got slapped with a £55 per person charge at the airport. Painful. Whoops Fund.
- We ran out of formula on a ridiculously expensive resort island in the Maldives and had to send a boat to a nearby island to buy some. Expensive Whoops Fund.
- I lost my only pair of prescription glasses in the sea while attempting a selfie on a pedal boat. You got it, the Whoops Fund had my unexpected contact lens purchase covered.

I could go on, but you get the idea. Just be prepared with your Whoops Fund OK? Worst-case scenario? You come home with more money than expected.

How much can you comfortably set aside each month? Based on that, how long will it take to reach the amount you need?

Keep your options open

Travelling in the shoulder season (the months either side of the peak season) can make a huge difference, often slashing costs and shortening your savings timeline. Many package holiday providers offer low- or even zero-deposit options, allowing you to secure a price and spread payments in interest-free instalments. This can make those bucket-list trips feel far more achievable.

Get the kids involved!

Not only does getting the kids involved make them feel more invested in the holiday, but it also teaches them valuable lessons about saving and budgeting. They could sell old clothes or toys on platforms like Vinted or eBay – or even help you declutter and list items you no longer need. Having a visible "family travel fund" can make saving more fun for them (think a white board or jar of money), and turning chores into contributions towards the fund might just make them a little more enthusiastic about tidying up!

Budget travel isn't about missing out – it's about spending smartly so you can travel more often. It's about knowing when to splurge and when to save (do you really need that private pool?). And, most importantly, it's about proving every smug naysayer wrong when they said you'd never travel again after having kids. Because trust me – the best adventures are yet to come.

Now that we've got your budget under control, it's time to tackle the next travel headache: getting there (and around) without remortgaging your house. In the next chapter, we'll dive into flights, transfers and all the little tricks to keep your transport costs firmly in the "bargain" zone.

BUDGET PLANNER

This table will help you plan the budget for your next few trips. If you're anything like me, having a visual representation makes everything feel a lot clearer. If you're booking a package holiday, your flights, hotel and transport will usually be included in one price. Then, using the tips in this chapter, you can figure out the other costs and see exactly how much you'll need to save.

	Trip 1	Trip 2	Trip 3	Trip 4
Flights				
Hotel				
Transport				
Food				
Activities				
Insurance				
Other				
TOTAL				

	Trip 5	Trip 6	Trip 7	Trip 8
Flights				
Hotel				
Transport				
Food				
Activities				
Insurance				
Other				
TOTAL				

Chapter Two
FLIGHTS AND TRANSPORT

I suppose you could say our family travel life *took off* the moment our son Leo arrived, though his entrance into the world was anything but low-key. The day before I went into hospital, in what can only be described as a questionable pre-departure decision, I'd planned a DIY glitter bath photoshoot. You know the kind – bump out, water dyed pink, glitter floating everywhere like you've been mugged by a unicorn. But not in a first-class roll-top bath, oh no. This was in our very much "economy" bathroom, with its cracked tiles and crumbling sealant. Because we'd now *upgraded* from my parents' attic to our very own house – a fixer-upper, which may or may not ever get "fixed up". There I was, 39 weeks pregnant, like a beached whale in a tepid, sparkly puddle, convinced this would look absolutely *brilliant* on the gram (spoiler alert: it most definitely did not make it to the gram – or anywhere else for that matter).

Fast forward 24 hours and I'm unexpectedly in the delivery room, legs akimbo, with a very confused-looking midwife peering down and gently asking, "Is there … glitter down here?" Honestly, nothing quite prepares you for the moment you have to explain to a medical professional why your labia is shimmering like a Christmas bauble mid-contraction. But hey – long story short, Leo arrived safe, sparkly and ready for adventure.

Within weeks, we were sorting out his first passport photo (trying to get a newborn to stay still and "look neutral" is always a laugh) and booking his first flight to see our family in Portugal. That was the start of it all – tiny passports, big bags and a whole lot of travel chaos that would go on to become the soundtrack to our lives. The good news? With a bit of planning, that chaos can be dialled down. This chapter is here to help – from choosing between package deals and DIY adventures to bagging affordable flights and navigating transport without the meltdown.

PACKAGE DEALS VERSUS DIY TRAVEL

Although there are pros and cons to both types of travel, we're personally big fans of the DIY approach. In fact, The Travel Mum was originally born out of my love for planning these kinds of trips. We built our website to make it easier for families to plan their own adventures without having to sell a kidney to afford them.

Package deals are popular for a reason. Flights, accommodation, and often transfers, are all bundled up in one neat little decision, which is why so many families opt for them. And with the chaos of family life, I get it. I understand why parents often want to land in the sun, be able to stick the kids in a club during happy hour and then return home with little to no decision-making needed along the way.

There are certain situations where package deals will win on value. Providers often offer free child places, and infants under two usually travel for free. There is a stage in family life – what I like to call the golden years – where you can book a package holiday and only pay for the grown-ups. If you have a one-year-old and a five-year-old, for example, they could technically both travel for free.

If you're looking for a classic all-inclusive holiday of 7, 10 or 14 nights in a popular tourist resort, 9 times out of 10 a package deal is your best bet. However, if you're craving something off the beaten track, a city break or a holiday with a duration outside the standard 7-, 10- or 14-night packages, booking DIY is often the smarter choice. People will automatically opt for a seven-night break, but that's not always ideal. During shorter school holiday periods, a five- or six-night getaway can be far more convenient. Likewise, a three-night city break over a long weekend can deliver all the benefits of travel without the hefty price tag or the need to sacrifice a big chunk of your annual leave.

Package deal pros
- Convenience
- Sometimes offer rep support on holiday
- Free child places
- Package travel regulations: help if something goes wrong
- ATOL/ABTA protection (for UK-based tour operators; basically, if a company goes bust, ATOL/ABTA will make sure you are refunded and/or repatriated. ATOL covers flight-based packages; ABTA covers non-flight-based travel)
- *Can* be cheaper (often with popular tourist resorts and all-inclusive bookings for 7, 10 and 14 nights)

DIY booking pros
- Greater flexibility: choice of more varied accommodation, durations and destinations not covered by your package provider
- More personalised experience
- Access to loyalty programmes and perks
- Easy to plan multi-destination trips
- Can explore lesser-known destinations
- *Can* be cheaper (with multi-destination trips, city breaks, certain places and durations outside of the typical 7-, 10- or 14-night stays)

People often miss out on cheaper, more flexible and often more interesting trips by swerving the DIY option. In the rest of this chapter, I will talk about how you can start to plan this type of trip, concentrating on flights and transport first.

FLIGHTS FIRST
When planning a flight-based DIY trip, the very first thing you need to tackle is the flight itself. If you're used to booking package holidays, this might be something you've never given much thought to – flights just *come with it*. But when you're doing it yourself, flight prices can vary dramatically from day to day. It might cost £20 to fly on a Thursday

and £200 the very next day. It could cost £100pp more to fly at midday as opposed to the 6am flight – which, if you're a family of four, is no joke! Research is key.

Accommodation, on the other hand, tends to keep its cool – prices usually stay pretty steady from one night to the next. So, if you've got any wiggle room in your plans, it's the flights that should dictate your dates. Golden rule: never, ever book your accommodation before you've sorted how you're actually getting there! (Unless it has free cancellation.)

Tools of the trade: The websites you need

When it comes to researching flights, you need a good comparison website in your corner, like Skyscanner, which searches smaller online travel agencies (OTAs) as well as the bigger companies, often finding the best prices. It's really user-friendly too – even my technophobe parents regularly use it. Google Flights is another brilliant tool. You can pull up a map showing where you can go and how much it'll cost, ideal for those "anywhere but here" moods. I also use it to track the price history of a flight, so you'll know whether the current fare is low, typical or high.

And – shameless plug incoming – I can't not mention The Travel Mum website here. Yes, I made it and yes, I'm biased, but it genuinely solves the problems we kept running into when planning our own DIY trips. The faffiest part of putting together your own holiday is finding cheap flights *and* accommodation that actually line up. Our DIY Trip Builder searches both at the same time, so you won't be stuck with bargain flights but nowhere decent to stay. It's especially handy for bigger families who need a lot of space and not just multiple hotel rooms. You can save your favourite trip combos, track the combined price and we'll email you if either the flights or hotel drop in price so that you can book at the right time. We've also built in a feature that lets you search within specific time periods. Most websites force you to pick an exact date or search the whole month, which isn't much use when you're tied to the Easter holidays or a specific two weeks of annual leave. On The Travel Mum, you can search *within* any dates you fancy, handy for the school holidays or finding the best long weekend trips.

Many people are now using AI to help them plan, which can be a great resource, but you need to double check the information it gives you. I have heard many stories of AI giving incorrect information, which you really don't need when you arrive at an airport at 11pm with kids!

THE BEST TIME TO BOOK

This is a topic people love to discuss. Whenever I am invited to chat on TV or radio, without fail, I am always asked, "So, when is the best time to book your flights?" And, like most things in travel, the answer is, annoyingly, not simple. You will hear people say, "Book on a Tuesday afternoon, in incognito mode, during a waxing gibbous moon ..." Sounds great for a snappy headline or one of those "quick tip" social media videos. But after over 15 years of scouring flights as my evening guilty pleasure, I haven't seen truth in any of it.

Although there's no magical booking time (sorry!), there *are* a few things you can do to avoid getting mugged off:

- Use a tool like Google Flights' price checker to see if the current price is low, typical or high.
- Find a credit card that allows you to earn points on everyday spending. You can then use these for cheaper flights or upgrades. We collect Avios points, which can be used with a variety of airlines.
- Set price alerts to monitor the price over a few weeks. With knowledge of the "typical" price, you should be able to work out when to swoop in.

- Avoid the "prime-time" scroll. Everyone else is searching flights on Sunday night when they're bored or feeling fed up about work the next day, so prices surge. Try weekday mornings instead, when nobody sane is browsing holidays.
- For short-haul flights (three hours or fewer), it is often cheapest within the one- to four-month period before the flight departs. It is rarely beneficial to book these flights too far in advance, *unless* it is for a very popular destination or period (festivals, events, Christmas, and so on).
- Don't leave it *too* late. Around a week before the flight departs, prices will typically go up a lot. Very last-minute bookings rarely save you money these days.
- Once you have paid for the flights, stop looking! If the price drops, you're going to spend the next three weeks fuming about that £10 difference. Let it go, save your sanity and start planning the rest of your holiday instead.

Flexibility is your secret weapon

Flexibility is your golden ticket if you want to bag those proper bargain prices. If you can save £400 by dragging yourself out of bed for the 6am flight, it's a no-brainer – get that coffee down you and crack on. The kids will no doubt cope better than you! Arriving early also means more time at the destination: it's a win-win.

We recently booked a trip to Sardinia and it turned out to be a grand cheaper to fly from London Gatwick instead of our local airport. Sure, it meant a 4-hour jaunt in the car each way instead of a 60-minute drive to our local, but for that kind of saving? You'd be mad not to. If we hadn't checked all of our options, we might have binned off the whole Sardinia idea thinking it was too pricey.

The key is knowing when a bit of extra effort is worth the reward. Sometimes, the savings aren't worth the hassle, but sometimes they absolutely are. Keep an open mind and weigh up the trade-offs. The same goes for *where* you go. If you fancy a beach break, does it really have to be *that* one resort in Spain? What if Portugal, Croatia or even Albania were dishing out the same sunshine and sangria vibes for half the price? For city breaks, get creative – hop on The Travel Mum website, search from your nearest airport to "any city" and see where you can jet off to within your budget. Sometimes, the best trips are the ones you didn't even have on your radar. *(See p94 for my hidden gem destinations.)*

> **TOP TIP**
> **Consider swapping the beach for a city break.**
> While everyone else is fighting over sunbeds in overpriced resorts, you could be tucking into picnics in shady parks, cooling off with a dip in a lake or unleashing the kids on a zoo or theme park. It's often a fraction of the cost of a beach holiday with less sensory overload. And if you do want that classic sunny escape, don't sleep on holiday camps. Think caravans with air con, splash pools, kids' clubs and evening entertainment that's brilliantly naff – all for a fraction of what you'd pay at a swanky hotel resort. The kids will love it, your wallet will love it and you might even surprise yourself and love it too!

Layover lessons: When is it worth it?

If you're flying long haul, you can save an absolute fortune by considering flights with layovers. And, honestly, the longer, more ridiculous and utterly inconvenient the route, the bigger the savings seem to be. We once found ourselves with a cheeky eight-hour stopover in Shanghai en route to Tokyo. This stopover followed a ten-hour flight with a wriggly toddler. And let me tell you – nothing, and I mean *nothing*, on this planet was going to convince me to "make the most of it" and head off sightseeing in Shanghai. Not a chance. We hunted down a quiet corner by a few toys (most airports will have a kids area and they are game changers) and let Leo go feral while we stared into the distance, clutching XL coffees and questioning our life choices.

If you've got older kids, a higher tolerance for chaos or you're a bit more adventurous than me at my most sleep-deprived, you can turn a long layover into a bonus mini city break. Just make sure the saving's worth the faff. If you've got a child who treats every airport like a personal assault course, maybe spend the extra money on a direct flight and save your last nerve for the holiday. In the case of our flights to Tokyo, we paid £1,800 to get to Tokyo and back with the Shanghai detour. Direct flights would have been around £4,000. The £2,200 saving paid for all of our accommodation on our three-week Japan trip, so the sacrifice was *just about* worth it – and somewhat character-building with hindsight.

Budget airline hidden costs

Right, let's talk about budget airline hidden costs – because if there's a way to squeeze an extra tenner out of you, they'll find it. The headline price always looks dreamy: "£19.99 flights to Milan", you click "book" and, before you know it, you've added seat selection, priority boarding, a check-in bag and a sandwich you don't actually want, and, somehow, it's now £200. Just slow down and reassess. That £19.99 flight *can* be £19.99 – you just have to learn the skill of packing light *(see box on p48)*, accept the fate of being sat away from other adults in your party (kids under 12 will very likely be sat with an adult regardless) and avoid everything they try to sell you en route to the checkout page. Easier said than done, I know.

Read the small print

Check the airline's baggage size and weight rules beforehand. These will be different for carry-on luggage (the things you are taking on board) and check-in luggage (the luggage you hand over to put in the hold). Carry-on luggage could be an under-seat bag (a rucksack, for example) or a small cabin suitcase. We have never been asked to "size" our rucksacks, but you often see epic battles break out about how big the carry-on suitcases are allowed to be. Make sure it's the right size and save yourself the drama. I say this having never travelled with the right size rucksack. We have been trying our luck with oversized bags for the last ten or more years and so far so good. We recently saw a check-in assistant charge a little old man for his slightly too big rucksack. My heart broke as he counted out the pound coins from his purse. The check-in lady then celebrated with her supervisor as she said, "Woo, my first time charging." The sensible travel advisor in me will tell you to be safe and take the right size bag. The rebel in me says, "just don't get caught …"

Screenshot everything
Budget airline apps have an uncanny habit of glitching exactly when you need them. It's always two minutes before the gate closes when your boarding pass mysteriously decides not to load … To dodge tech dramas at the gate, screenshot your boarding passes or download them to your phone's digital wallet. When booking flights with third parties, I *always* screenshot the booking confirmation screen, just in case the confirmation email doesn't come through and I need to tackle the final boss (aka travel agency customer service).

BYO snacks (and bottles!)
Airport snacks are no joke. I saw a £2 Milky Bar at the airport the other day. Not a big share bar – oh no, it was the paper-thin rectangle bar you find lurking in the bottom of Christmas selection boxes. Save a small fortune by bringing your own snacks and an empty reusable water bottle. Most airports have free water stations after security.

Prepay for extras (only if essential)
If you genuinely need a checked bag or seat selection, book it online in advance. It's always pricier last minute or at the airport.

Don't fall for insurance upsells
Budget airlines often push their own insurance in a way that implies you *need* it. You do 100 per cent need travel insurance (*p28*), but it is very likely going to be cheaper elsewhere. As mentioned earlier, check first whether you're already covered by your bank, home insurance or a separate annual travel insurance policy. If you need insurance, use comparison websites to get the right policy for you.

Check in baby items or pushchairs

Budget airlines love to keep things vague, and baby gear is no exception. Most of them let you check in two items per child – think pram, car seat, travel cot – completely free. But, of course, they don't shout about it. In fact, you'll often see an option for "baby items" pop up during booking, which feels like a personal attack on sleep-deprived parents just trying to do the right thing. Don't panic and don't add it on. Just rock up to the airport with your gear and check it in at the desk – no drama, no extra cost (just triple-check the airline's policy first as some do only allow one item).

PACKING LIGHT

Packing light is one of the easiest ways to save money – it will save you a fortune over the years – but it's something many families (understandably) struggle with. The instinct is to pack for *every possible scenario*: three changes of clothes per day, a pharmacy aisle's worth of "just in case" medicines and cosmetics, and enough toys to open your own kids' club. But unless you want to blow your budget on baggage fees (and your back on cobbled streets), it's time to learn the art of travelling lean.

Here's how to do it without feeling like you've left half your life at home:
- **Choose your bags wisely:** If your flights include free under-seat luggage, make it work for you. A small rucksack per person often beats one giant suitcase you all have to share (and argue over). If you have a package holiday

planned that includes luggage, pick a suitcase that will allow you to make the most of your allowance.
- **Roll, don't fold:** To roll or to fold? It's one of travel's biggest controversies. I am *all* for rolling. It's a no-brainer, especially when packing a rucksack. Not only does rolling clothes save space, it also avoids the "I've slept in a hedge" look when you unpack.
- **Mix-and-match:** Pick a simple colour palette so everything goes together. That way, four items magically become a week's worth of outfits.
- **Shoes – keep them minimal:** Two pairs max per person – one comfy, one nice. Shoes eat luggage allowance faster than kids eat holiday ice cream. Wear your bulkiest pair on the plane.
- **Mini everything:** Toiletries, gadgets, toys. Decant liquids into travel bottles, bring a Kindle instead of a pile of books and let the kids pick *one* favourite toy each (plus the emotional-support teddy, obvs).
- **Use packing cubes:** You can really condense your clothes in these and they are great for rucksacks and suitcases. They're basically drawers for your suitcase. One cube per person = no more panicked rummaging for clean pants at midnight.
- **Laundry over luggage:** Instead of packing extra outfits, choose accommodation with a washing machine (or even just a sink, and take some travel wash with you). One wash mid-week means you can halve the clothes you take with you.
- **Multipurpose heroes:** Sarongs, muslins or big scarves can be beach towels, picnic blankets, shade or makeshift baby wraps. Who doesn't want to mooch around all day wearing a shawl?
- **Wear the bulkiest stuff:** Hoodies, trainers, winter coats – if it takes up space, wear it to the airport. You can strip off once you're through security. We did this when we visited Lapland for a week with carry-on luggage.

Getting to your accommodation from the airport

Ah, the airport transfer – the bit that's often blissfully handled for you on a package holiday. A cheerful rep waves you over, your name's on a list and a coach with air con and questionable curtains whisks you off without a care in the world. Dreamy ... when it works out.

With a DIY trip? Not *quite* the same story – and I know this puts off a lot of people travelling this way. But, honestly, once you've done it a couple of times, it's really no big deal. You just need your plan locked in *before* you arrive, or risk standing outside Arrivals, child on one hip, three bags on the other, frantically googling "Does Uber work in [insert wherever you are]?"

Trust me, I've lived the drama. A taxi is rarely the cheapest option, but sometimes it's the only thing your last nerve can handle – and that's OK. Just know your options, plan ahead and save the chaos for something more fun – like getting the kids to chill out when you finally get to your hotel room. Here's the lowdown:

- **Public transport:** This can be the cheapest option, especially in big cities, but it's worth checking timings to get the right bus or train – dragging bags and kids through three train changes at 9pm isn't the holiday vibe.
- **Shuttles and airport buses:** These are usually direct and good value, especially if booked ahead. Look at services like National Express, FlixBus or dedicated airport coaches. Airports that are located far away from the centre usually have these. Again, make sure departure times will work and have a plan B.
- **Car hire:** This can make sense if you're heading somewhere rural or if you plan to explore. It can often be cheaper than booking a return private transfer and means you will potentially save money on transport once at your destination. We prefer planning our own DIY excursions in a hire car over organised tours. For us, being able to run with our own schedule is essential when we have little ones. We'll look at car hire in more detail in Chapter Five, *p106*.

The key is to compare everything ahead of time – and, if in doubt, ask yourself, "Will I want to be figuring this out with hungry kids and no phone signal after a three-hour flight?" If the answer's no, sort it now!

ALTERNATIVES TO FLYING

Of course, flying isn't the only way to get from A to B – and sometimes it's not the best way. Trains, ferries, coaches and good old-fashioned road trips all deserve a moment in the spotlight. Not only can they work out cheaper (especially for short-haul trips), but they're also often greener and far less faff when you factor in the airport chaos. We have driven from the UK to France, Belgium and the Netherlands before. Being able to throw everything in the car without worrying about luggage allowances is a dream. Plus, for the kids, these journeys feel like part of the adventure – not just the boring bit before the holiday starts.

Trains mean window seats and snack trolleys. Ferries mean wind-in-your-hair deck runs and spotting sharks (or at least pretending to). And long car rides? If you're being optimistic, that's quality family time with 37 snack stops and a dodgy playlist ("Raining Tacos" is currently a fave in our car; if you know, you know ...). If you have a kid who gets car sick, then I wish you luck. The key is weighing up the pros and cons for your specific trip. Sometimes avoiding the plane altogether can save you money and stress, and do a bit for the planet too.

Interrailing in Europe

An interrail pass lets you hop between cities and even countries using the train, and can be cheaper than you think with family discounts and little kids often travelling for free. With so many different passes to choose from (single-country, multi-country, flexible dates), you can tailor your trip to suit your plans and budget. Always do your homework, though, as passes can require additional charges like seat reservations on some lines. Pair it with budget-friendly accommodation like hostels, family-run guesthouses or apartment stays, and you've got yourself a low-cost, high-fun adventure!

Ferry and road trip combos

If you're UK-based, especially near the south coast, hopping on a ferry to France can be a budget-friendly way to kick-start an adventure. Within a couple of hours, you're across the Channel and cruising through northern France – no baggage fees, no airport chaos, just you, the car and a boot full of everything you could ever need. Find a family-friendly holiday park (there are loads with pools, playgrounds and evening entertainment), and explore the region at your own pace. You could even squeeze in a day trip to Disneyland Paris if you're feeling fancy *(see p134 for my tips on visiting theme parks)*. It's a fun, flexible and affordable way to see a new country – just with a mild risk of divorce while trying to navigate French road signs.

Overnight coach trips

Lots of coach companies offer overnight routes to faraway places, which are great for adventurous families with older kids – just remember to bring a neck pillow and your sense of humour.

Mini cruises

Fancy a bit of sea air with your city break? Ferry companies like DFDS and P&O offer mini cruises from the UK to places like Amsterdam or Rotterdam. Most countries with a coast will offer something similar. You get a comfy cabin and entertainment, with the added bonus of waking up in another country. Many of these cruises will give you a day in the new country, and then bring you home. Perfect for a quick weekend getaway.

Cycling holidays

Hear me out: if your kids are a bit older or you've got a bike trailer for the little one, cycling trips can be a fun, active and affordable way to explore. Whichever country you are based in, there will no doubt be some beautiful routes to explore. Routes like the Loire Valley in France or Danube River in Austria are flat, scenic and peppered with amazing view stops. Book a few budget-friendly beds along the way and, suddenly, the journey *is* the holiday – Lycra optional.

The glitter-soaked start to our parenting journey pretty much set the tone for the kind of family travel we'd end up loving – a little chaotic, occasionally ridiculous, but always fabulous.

Planning your own flights and transfers might feel daunting at first, especially if you're used to the hand-holding of package holidays (which, don't get me wrong, absolutely have their place in your travel arsenal). But once you've done the DIY option a couple of times, it becomes second nature. And in return? You get more freedom, more flexibility and often a lot more holiday for your money.

With the right tools, a touch of flexibility and a big dose of humour, you'll be breezing through DIY bookings like a pro. Yes, it might take a bit more thought, but it also gives you so much more choice, adventure and value for money. Remember: it doesn't have to be perfect. It just has to work for *you*. Whether that means waking the kids up for a 6am bargain flight, taking the scenic ferry route to France or splurging on a taxi because you just-can't-anymore, you're doing it, and that's what matters! You've got this – glitter, chaos and all.

In the next chapter, we're diving into where you're going to stay – and, more importantly, how to make your accommodation work *hard* for your budget. Whether you're dreaming of a beachfront hotel, a cosy cabin in the woods or a no-frills apartment that lets you spend more money on ice cream than lodging, I've got you covered.

NEURODIVERSE FAMILIES: WHAT TO KNOW

Travelling as a neurodiverse family can be challenging, but with the right planning (and a bit of backup), it's absolutely doable – and enjoyable!

Many airports and airlines now offer extra support if you know what to ask for. One simple but powerful tool is the Hidden Disabilities Sunflower lanyard. Wearing one signals to staff that someone in your group may need a bit of extra time, patience or support – without having to explain everything at every step. You can usually request one in advance from the airport or pick one up at special assistance desks.

Airlines and airports vary, but lots now offer things like priority boarding, quiet waiting areas and even pre-travel familiarisation visits. Check their websites or contact customer services before you book – don't be shy about asking what accommodations they can offer. Some airlines also allow you to notify them of additional needs during the booking process.

Here are some booking tips for neurodiverse families:
- **Try to travel during quieter times:** Midweek flights plus early mornings are often less hectic.
- **Avoid tight layovers or short connection times where possible:** A more relaxed pace makes a huge difference.
- **Consider paying for fast-track security if available:** It can be worth it just to avoid sensory overload queues. Some airports will even allow people with hidden disabilities to use dedicated lanes.
- **Pack comfort items:** Bring noise-cancelling headphones, fidget toys or anything else that helps you or your child feel more calm and secure.

With a bit of prep and the right support, travel can feel less overwhelming and more empowering for everyone in the family – and that's what it's all about. At The Travel Mum, we have an autism-friendly holiday specialist who shares lots of great tips on her social media page and on our website, so it's worth checking that out too.

Chapter Three
BEDS ON A BUDGET

Our first family trip as a trio – after our trip to visit family in Portugal – was a real eye-opener. Gone were the extra pairs of hands, the fully equipped house and the ability to cry in peace while someone else held the baby. When we found ourselves on our own, out in the wild, just the two of us and this dependent little human, things were very different. The trip started with me whacking the poor little fella's head on a taxi door as I clambered out, three bags in my arms, baby strapped to my front, sweating like I'd just ran a marathon ... I cried more than Leo did. We got to our apartment and it didn't have a cot – which really didn't matter as he was yet to sleep away from my boobs but, at the time, it seemed like a big deal. The air con didn't work, the room smelled of smoke and the bedroom had two tiny single beds. Could we push them together? Yes. Did I do that instead of having a meltdown? Absolutely not.

It only takes a couple of mini disasters to make you question the entire trip. But I've learned the cure: get everyone washed, fed and cool, and maybe sneak in a glass of wine. Before you know it, your nervous system will have chilled out and you'll be ready to enjoy your holiday. In the situation above, João spoke to Reception (while I sat and cried) and we were able to change rooms to a cooler and less smelly one – they even brought us a cot that we didn't use once. All was good.

Choosing the right accommodation is everything – and, honestly, it's my favourite part to plan. Some people scroll Rightmove for houses they'll never buy; I scroll hotel listings for holidays I'm not even going on. I read *everything*: TripAdvisor, Facebook groups, even the hotel's allergy and accessibility guides. Got a bad review? I'm stalking the reviewer like Sherlock Holmes with a Wi-Fi connection.

Are they legit? Were they in a bad mood because they whacked their baby's head on a car door on arrival? Are they a serial one-star-er with a vendetta against holidays? Because let's be real – travel is subjective, and some people just hate fun.

Despite all this Sherlock-level sleuthing, I'm actually really chill when it comes to where *we* stay. It makes no sense, I know. You'll catch me tutting about a new five-star resort not having a hoist by the pool, then, two minutes later, booking a no-star guesthouse in the middle of nowhere. My logic? It's all about finding the *best possible option* for our family and our budget. The "right" accommodation for you will likely not be right for me. And what's right for me now is very different to what worked for me ten years ago. Things change. Budgets change. Children appear.

These days, my decisions are mostly driven by practicality and value. If one hotel is £5 more per night but includes breakfast, that will save us spending on breakfast each day (and prevent a daily drama of finding somewhere to eat that suits everyone). But always check the reviews first – because not all hotel breakfasts are created equal. Parking is another big one to consider: free parking at one hotel versus £20 a day at another? That's a huge saving over a week-long holiday. Basically, it's never just about choosing the cheapest option on paper – it's about choosing the *smartest* one.

Now, I haven't always been this savvy. My first big trip (planned poorly, might I add) was to Thailand when I was 18. We'd had a tough time as a family, and I'd dropped out of my first year of medical school (spoiler: I did eventually go back). Most people would have processed things with therapy or a new hobby. I booked a three-month solo trip to Thailand. I'd just lost my grandad, who left me some money, and I figured a wild adventure was exactly what I needed (and, with hindsight, it absolutely was). I didn't research anything properly – my idea of "preparing" was taking a 2p Ryanair flight to Dublin to "practise flying alone" (I'm giving away my age with those flight prices!). I bought a sheep keyring in Dublin city centre and flew back the same day. Job done. I was ready for Asia.

The Thailand trip ended up being wildly chaotic, underprepared and completely life-changing. I stayed in 20p beach huts (continuing to date myself, but, yes, this was nearly 20 years ago), crashed in hostels, slept on night ferries, even on the beach a couple of times. Accommodation was a practicality, nothing more. I needed somewhere cheap, safe-ish and *ideally* not swarming with mosquitoes. That's it. And, honestly, that's all you *really* need, most of the time. During the trip, there were naturally lots of near-misses – I left with lots of bizarre stories, and I ended up on an infectious diseases ward on my return home, but that's a story for another time!

Those scrappy nights in Thailand, along with my experience of living in the Scottish wilderness, taught me that you really can get by and see the world on even the tightest budget. It also taught me that luxury is overrated – the best parts of travel come from the experience, not the room you sleep in. And while I now travel with more people (and more wet wipes), that mindset hasn't changed. Clean, comfy and safe is the baseline – everything else is an unnecessary bonus. Fast forward a decade (or so) and my travel life looks *a bit* different. But the mission's still the same: maximise adventure, minimise cost and always make the most of the breakfast buffet. These days, I've got more tools and tricks (and comparison sites) at my disposal – and, in this chapter, I'm going to share them with you.

Ready to find the perfect place to stay (without needing a second job to pay for it)? Let's get into it!

SELF-CATERING VERSUS ALL-INCLUSIVE: WHAT'S RIGHT FOR YOU?

If you're travelling with kids (especially small ones or fussy eaters), choosing between self-catering and all-inclusive options can feel like a tough choice. So, let's start by looking at the pros and cons of each.

Self-catering: The budget-saver's dream

Self-catering accommodation is perfect for picky eaters, beige food lovers and budget-conscious families. You eat in your PJs and no one judges you for feeding the kids cereal three times a day. When we self-cater, we shop at local supermarkets, cook simple meals and use the money we save on actual fun things like boat trips, ice creams and replacing glasses lost at sea. It also lets you create your own chilled vibe. No one is judging your parenting when the kids won't chill out. YouTube over dinner? Anything for the peace. And the balcony wine and 'picky bits' nights after the kids' bedtime? Chef's kiss.

Now, you don't have to scrimp on every meal – we will often prepare breakfast and dinner ourselves, and treat ourselves to a nice lunch out during the day. As I've mentioned, lunch menus are often a lot cheaper than dinner menus and it means you still get to try yummy local food.

On the downside, you do have to cook (or at least assemble things). And without a dishwasher (partner or machine), you have to do the washing up. Also, if you are staying in an apartment that isn't within a resort-style complex, there may not be an entertainment team distracting your kids with the "Macarena" while you collapse into a sangria in peace. Sometimes, you want to go away and do absolutely nothing, and that's OK.

> **TOP TIP**
> **Find a balance between cheap and cheerful dinners and a splash of local food fun.**
> To avoid the feeling of "just doing life but in a different country", plan a few ultra-easy meal nights (I've shared some easy ideas at the end of this chapter, *p74*), and also allow for some meals out when you haven't got the will to cook.

All-inclusive: The stress-free option (sometimes)

Want zero food-related decisions for a week? Then all-inclusive it is. Your kids are constantly fed, drinks are flowing and you don't have to wash a single dish. Predicting and planning food costs is simpler too.

But not all all-inclusive hotels are equal. Some have gourmet buffets. Others? Beige mush and mystery meat. Always check the reviews – things like Facebook groups, TripAdvisor and even social media can show what's *actually* going on.

Look out for hidden extras too – not all resorts include snacks or branded drinks in the all-inclusive price. Certain activities could be excluded as well. And if your kids aren't big eaters or you plan to be out exploring most days, you might end up paying for meals that you never eat, which is wasteful and expensive.

So what's best?
- If you're on a tight budget with picky eaters and are willing to do some DIY dining, go self-catering.
- If you want ease, predictability and a decision-free holiday, all-inclusive could be the way.
- If you want somewhere in between, look into half-board packages or places with kitchenettes and on-site dining, giving you the option to easily do both.

FACTORS TO CONSIDER: FINDING WHAT ACTUALLY WORKS FOR YOUR FAMILY

Choosing the right accommodation isn't just about ticking boxes – it's about avoiding holiday meltdowns before they happen (and I don't just mean from the kids).

There's no "one size fits all" when it comes to accommodation. What works for a family of five with three teenagers is going to be very different from what works for a solo parent travelling with a toddler and a suitcase full of nappies. Bad reviews are going to happen for most hotels, so don't immediately be put off by these, especially if, like us, you are quite laid back. A hotel could have a bad review for being too quiet, but this may be perfect for someone else. Someone may leave a bad review for the pool being closed, which might not be the case when you arrive. I have seen bad reviews for the most ridiculous things, like it being too windy, or the pool being too cold in November ... Reviews are important, but always take them with a pinch of salt and make your own decisions. Remember that people are much more likely to go online to leave a bad review than make the effort to leave a good one.

Here are the key things to think about before you book:

Family size and sleeping arrangements

It sounds obvious, but make sure there are enough beds. Not just technically enough beds, but *comfortable* sleeping setups. Some rooms will say they are appropriate for a family of four, but only have one small double bed (this happened a lot on a recent trip to Japan). A sofa bed might seem fine in the listing, but try sharing it with a sweaty six-year-old who kicks in his sleep and you might rethink everything.

Consider whether you want a separate room for the kids, and check if cots or extra beds are available for little ones (and at what cost). This is especially important in countries where hotels typically accommodate fewer people per room than we're used to in the UK. Families of five or more will often be split into two hotel rooms, which can end up costing a fortune. It also isn't ideal with a young family, but *can* be perfect if travelling with teens who want their own space. Bigger families can cut costs by looking at two- and three-bedroom apartments or even private villas.

Location, location, sanity

Think about your trip style. Are you planning beach days? City exploring? National parks? Being within walking distance of what you'll be doing most can save a *ton* of hassle. Even the best-value property starts to feel less of a bargain if you're spending £30 a day on buses or losing hours to traffic and tantrums. Also check:
- Is the area family-friendly?
- Are there pavements and crossings if you've got a buggy?
- Is it hilly?

- Are there a gazillion steps to get to the hotel?
- Will it feel safe coming back late from dinner or a sunset walk?

And yes, proximity to a decent coffee shop may not be essential for all, but for many of us it's a sanity-saver. Being close to attractions, a beach, public transport or even just a decent supermarket can save you time, money and meltdowns. A slightly more expensive place *in* town can often work out better value than a cheaper option that's miles out and requires a taxi every time someone wants an ice cream.

Amenities

Not all heroes wear capes. Some come in the form of a washing machine, a microwave or a plug socket near the bed. When you're travelling with kids, the little things become the big things.

Don't assume anything – listings can be vague, and what counts as "kitchen facilities" might just be a kettle and a rusty spoon. Look for listings that show clear photos of the amenities or list them in detail, and make sure the photos you are seeing are actually of the room you are booking. Reviewers are always quick to point out when a kitchen is sparse. And if something is going to be a deal-breaker for you, email the host to double-check before you book. Below are those amenities that, for us, make life easier:

- **Kitchen/kitchenette:** I've already covered this, but it's a must-have for budget-conscious families. Note that many kitchenettes may only have a two-ring hob with no oven or microwave (*I've included some meal ideas for situations like this on p74*).
- **Washing machine:** This is essential for longer stays or when you inevitably run out of clean pants halfway through. If we're travelling for two weeks or more, we often wash our clothes halfway through the holiday to prevent having to bring our whole wardrobe with us.
- **Microwave:** Ideal for heating up milk, pasta or that half-eaten dinner your toddler insisted they hated and now loves again 40 minutes later.

- **Dishwasher:** This is by no means essential, but it is definitely a perk. No washing up = more time for actual fun (or staring at a wall in silence once the kids are asleep).
- **Wi-Fi:** This is especially important if your kids need screens for downtime (or if you plan to work while you're away).
- **Baby equipment:** Think high chairs, travel cots, stair gates ... Feeding a one-year-old without being able to strap them into a chair is an Olympic-level test of patience, balance and reflexes you didn't know you had.
- **Blackout curtains/shutters:** These are *gold dust* if you've got little ones with early sleep schedules – or if you just want a lie-in and don't fancy a sunrise wake-up at 5.12am. I'm always *very* interested in the curtain setup within our rooms!

Safety and accessibility

It might not be the sexiest part of holiday planning, but, if you're travelling with kids, elderly relatives or anyone with additional needs, safety and accessibility checks are non-negotiable. A dreamy balcony view isn't worth much if your toddler can squeeze through the bars or your nan can't make it up the stairs. Below are some things to think about before you book (based on lessons learned the hard way):

General safety
- **Is the pool fenced or gated?** You'd be surprised how many private villas don't have *any* barrier around the pool. If you've got kids who run before they think, this one's vital.
- **Are the balconies child-safe?** Look at the height of the railing, the gaps between bars and whether furniture could be used as a climbing frame. Assume your child *will* try to scale it.
- **Do windows open fully?** Check if they have locks or restrictors. Not all countries follow the same safety standards – don't assume.
- **What's the nearest indoor option for bad weather?** Check if there's a library, soft play or museum nearby for escape-the-rain days – this isn't technically a safety tip, but *absolutely* a sanity one.

Emergency preparedness
- **Where's the nearest hospital or urgent care?** Save the name, address and directions *before* you need them.
- **What's the local emergency number?** Not everywhere uses 999. Learn the local equivalent (for example, 112 in Europe).
- **Is there a fire extinguisher and smoke alarm?** This is especially important in self-catering properties with kitchens, BBQs or fireplaces. (Look, I'm not saying you're going to burn the sausages and set fire to the place, but, if you do …)

Accessibility considerations
- **Is the accommodation on one level or accessible by lift?** Many charming properties = many stairs and *no lift*. Check in advance. We (aka João) recently had to carry our luggage, the baby and our chunky pram up *four* flights of stairs …
- **Are paths and entrances paved and wide enough?** Cobblestones might look cute on Instagram, but try pushing a pram or wheelchair over them – vibration injury is a real thing I'm sure I've experienced!
- **Is there accessible parking nearby?** If someone in your party needs to limit walking distance, this can make or break a stay.
- **Are showers walk-in or over a bath?** Some bathroom setups may not work for your needs – that stylish claw-foot tub might be a nightmare for anyone with mobility issues. Check the photos for accessible bathrooms.

Whether you're travelling with a buggy, mobility aid or just trying to avoid hauling everything up a mountain of stairs, for accessibility, think beyond just wheelchair access. Is the property single-storey? Does it have high beds that might be tricky for some people? Many properties now include accessibility info, but, if not, again, just ask. Hosts who care won't mind answering your questions. Check for stair gates, balcony safety, gated pools and ground-floor access if you're travelling with little ones or anyone with mobility needs. Not all properties are childproof, and you don't want to spend your holiday on edge.

> **TOP TIP**
> **Do a vibe check.**
> Some places are just more family-friendly than others. Does the listing mention that families or children are welcome? Are there toys, books or a playground on site? If a host has gone to the effort of adding family-friendly features, that's usually a good sign they get it.

CREATIVE ACCOMMODATION OPTIONS

If you've only ever stayed in hotels or Airbnbs, let me open your eyes to a whole world of possibilities. When you start getting creative with your accommodation, you don't just save money, you also get better stories. ("Remember that time we slept in a converted train carriage?" beats "We paid £300 a night for a beige room with no kettle" any day.)

House-sitting

This is one of my favourite budget travel hacks. House-sitting means you stay in someone's home – often for free – in exchange for looking after their house, pets or plants. It's perfect if you're flexible with dates and love animals (or like the idea of pretending to live in someone else's life for a bit), and often you get to stay in lovely homes, with kitchens, gardens and sometimes even pools. We have done lots of house-sits and the home owners often leave food and alcohol for us to enjoy (The Ritz would *never*).

There are websites that connect families with homeowners, and you can find everything from countryside cottages to city flats. Most gigs involve pet care, so it's not ideal if you're allergic to cats, but brilliant if your kids love animals. However, you need to be reliable, flexible and OK with the occasional early-morning dog walk. That being said, there are a huge variety of animals, and lots of sites allow you to filter by the ones you are happy to care for.

Hostels

"Hostels for families?" I hear you ask. Yes, really. Hostels have come a *long* way from the sticky-floored dens of my Thailand adventure days.

Many now offer private family rooms, en-suite bathrooms, kitchens, play areas and even on-site cafés. They're usually super central and way cheaper than hotels. They often include breakfast too.

In terms of the downsides, some hostels will have shared bathrooms, thin walls or a general "youth vibe", but the trade-off can be worth it if you're saving £100+ a night. Shared bathrooms are usually less gross than you think. We stayed in a hostel once that had shared bathrooms. You might imagine everyone showering together, but that isn't the case. In our particular hostel, there were five individual bathrooms, which were cleaned after every use. Our whole family could go into the bathroom, lock the door behind us and do what we had to do. There was only us and one other family staying there too.

If you're tempted, look for hostels that specifically mention families and read the reviews to make sure it's not a stag-do haven. If you are a big family, look out for options for three- to six-bed private rooms or consider booking out an entire dorm, which is a cheap way to ensure you all sleep together.

Holiday rentals and apartments

This is your classic Airbnb setup – still a top choice for families, especially for longer stays. Look out for properties that offer weekly discounts, and don't be afraid to message the hosts directly to ask about deals or kid-friendly extras.

> **TOP TIP**
> **Use the map feature on booking platforms.**
> This will ensure you're not accidentally booking a "ten-minute walk to town" that's actually halfway up a mountain. Descriptions can be very creative! Most accommodation booking sites will let you look at a map and view hotels based on their location – much easier than viewing them in a list with no idea where each one is.

Camping and holiday parks

These are ideal if your kids love the outdoors and you don't mind the odd bug. From tents and glamping pods to mobile homes and static caravans, there's an option for every comfort level and budget. Holiday parks often come with pools, entertainment and kid-friendly activities. There's a whole chapter on this later (*p140*).

Narrowboat holidays
Why just stay *by* the water when you could live *on* it? A narrowboat along the canals of the UK (or even in parts of Europe) turns your accommodation into a floating adventure. You cook on board, moor up in new places each day and the kids can learn how to open canal locks (free entertainment right there). Bonus: nobody can run away when they get in a strop!

B&Bs
They might sound a bit old-school, but B&Bs can be great for families. They're often cheaper than hotels, often come with a hearty breakfast that sets you up for the day, and you get the personal touch from the hosts.

Treehouses and cabins
Nothing says "best holiday ever" to a child than sleeping in a treehouse. These are popping up everywhere from the UK to European forests. We stayed in a treehouse when in Thailand and it was just as exciting for the adults!

FINDING THE BEST DEALS
Finding great accommodation deals isn't about getting lucky, it's about knowing where (and when) to look, and what to avoid. Here's how to play the game like a pro:

Booking in advance versus last-minute deals
There's a sweet spot depending on where you are planning to visit. Booking too far in advance can mean you miss out on last-minute discounts, but leaving it too late can mean everything decent is gone (or eye-wateringly expensive):

LOYALTY SCHEMES AND MEMBERSHIP PERKS

If you do tend to stay in hotels, you can do well from using the same platform. We love Hotels.com and find their One Key rewards programme adds up quickly. Bonuses can then be used to book future hotels and flights. Booking.com has a loyalty programme called Genius, offering perks such as free breakfast, room upgrades and special discounts as you climb up the rankings. Lots of hotel booking websites have their own loyalty perks, so work out which is best for you.

- **Advance booking:** Securing your accommodation in advance works well for school holidays, peak seasons or popular destinations where demand is high. It's also useful if you want more time to save. Many hotels will let you pay on arrival.
- **Last-minute:** Leaving things until closer to your departure date is perfect if you're flexible, spontaneous and a bit of a gambler. If you're an "anywhere cheap" kind of traveller, last-minute bookings are great (and this is how we like to travel!).
- **Booking with free cancellation:** This means you can book ahead of time, but have the option to cancel and rebook if the price drops (or if you find something better).

Direct booking versus third parties

Booking directly with the hotel or host can often score you extra perks like free breakfast, room upgrades or early check-in. It also helps small businesses avoid paying commission fees to the comparison websites.

But third-party sites (such as Booking.com, Hotels.com, Agoda, and so on) can be brilliant for comparing prices and filtering exactly what you want – like the number of beds, free cancellation, baby baths, and so on. As discussed, they also offer loyalty perks for regular bookings, which can sometimes beat the direct offer from the hotel.

For the best of both worlds, find a place you like on a comparison site, then check the hotel's website directly or even email them. Politely ask if they'll match the price or offer extras for booking directly. You'll be amazed how often they say yes. We did this with a booking in the Maldives and they agreed to make our "breakfast included" booking a half-board stay if we cancelled with the third-party site and booked directly with them. Luckily, we had free cancellation so were able to do this without incurring additional charges.

WATCH OUT FOR HIDDEN FEES

That dreamy £70-a-night apartment might look like a steal – until they add a £100 cleaning fee, £50 for Wi-Fi and a £25 towel charge. Always read the fine print. Look for total prices including fees before committing.

Tourist tax

Before travelling, check whether you'll have to pay tourist tax and if it is included in the price or something you will need to pay on arrival (this is more likely).

Check cancellation policies carefully

Life happens. Kids get sick. Plans change. Booking a rate with free cancellation might cost a bit more upfront, but it can save you big time if you need to switch things around. Once again, read the small print – some "free cancellation" deals only refund part of the cost or require you to cancel a week or more in advance.

Compare DIY versus packages

Always do a final comparison before committing to anything. Sometimes it's cheaper to book your hotel and flights separately. Other times, a package deal (like those on TUI and Jet2holidays) works out much better value – especially if transfers, meals or luggage are included.

Comparison is key. I always run the numbers both ways – separate bookings versus package – before committing.

Feeling like a booking boss yet? You should be.

Accommodation can make or break a trip – not just because of the number of beds or bathrooms, but because of how it supports (or ruins) your budget, your plans and your peace of mind. Make savvy choices, read the small print and remember: no one ever came home from holiday and said, "I wish we'd spent more money on that hotel."

So, you've mastered where to sleep – now let's decide where to go.

SELF-CATERING MEAL IDEAS

Let's talk about self-catering – just because you're not going out to eat, it doesn't mean dinner has to be dull. However, often the kitchens on holiday are *limited*, so if you find yourself with a two-ring hob and a few spoons, here are some quick and easy ideas for getting everyone fed – and, most importantly, without spending a fortune or three hours of your evening cooking!

- **Tuna pasta bake:** The classic. If there's no oven, don't panic – just mix cooked pasta with a tin of tuna, sweetcorn, chopped tomatoes and cheese, then serve it hot and gooey. Bonus points if you have a grill and can crisp it up on top.
- **Fajitas:** Sizzle some chicken or veggies with a fajita seasoning sachet, whack it into wraps and serve with cheese and whatever else you can find in the local supermarket.
- **Spag bol:** Cook the pasta on one ring, and the mince and sauce on the other. Feel smug when the kids wolf it down and you realise you've just saved £40 not eating at the beachside tourist trap.
- **Picky bits:** Also known as "Mum's night off". Bread, cheese, ham, olives, crisps, cherry tomatoes … lay it all out like a Mediterranean buffet and tell the kids it's "tapas".
- **Creamy pesto pasta:** Boil pasta, stir in cream cheese and some pesto, chuck in some cherry tomatoes or frozen peas. Minimum effort, maximum yum.

- **Stir-fry noodles:** Fry pre-chopped veggies with soy sauce and throw in some instant noodles. Add tofu or chicken if you're feeling fancy.
- **Tortellini with sauce:** Fresh tortellini boils in three minutes. Mix it with a jar of sauce or olive oil, garlic and any cheese that hasn't been stolen by the ants.
- **Chilli con carne:** Mince, chopped tomatoes, a tin of beans, maybe a stock cube if you're feeling chefy. Serve with rice. Easy.
- **Sausages and couscous:** Cook sausages, prepare couscous (just add boiling water!), and serve with tinned ratatouille or a side salad.
- **Risotto:** Stir stock into rice with frozen mushrooms and onions. It takes patience and wine – which, let's be honest, you were opening anyway.
- **Gnocchi:** Gnocchi in a frying pan with garlic, butter, spinach and cheese = cheat-day heaven.
- **Omelettes:** Eggs, cheese, ham, tomato – basically a fridge clear-out with flair. Serve with bread, salad or crisps (I won't judge).
- **Quesadillas:** Sandwich cheese and beans between two wraps, toast in a dry frying pan and cut into wedges. Tell the kids it's Mexican pizza.
- **Stuffed peppers:** Cook rice, mix it with tinned tuna, tomatoes and cheese, stuff into halved peppers and steam or cover and cook gently in a pan. Looks fancy, takes 12 minutes.
- **Greek salad and garlic bread:** Chop tomatoes, cucumber, onion, olives and feta, drizzle with oil. Warm up some garlic bread and enjoy with a glass of wine while pretending you're in *Mamma Mia*.

MY PLANNING CHECKLIST

Have you done everything you need to?

- ☐ Booked flights
- ☐ Booked accommodation
- ☐ Planned transport from the airport to the hotel
- ☐ Booked travel insurance
- ☐ Bought eSIM or turned off data roaming (if not included in your plan)
- ☐ Planned your spending money budget for the trip
- ☐ Filed your documents in a holiday folder, whether physical or electronic
- ☐ Checked your passport expiry date and the entry requirements for the country you're travelling to
- ☐ Considered how you will spend (credit card / prepaid card)

My Planning Checklist

Extra bits to think about:

- [ ] Applied for visas (if needed – don't get caught out at the gate!)
- [ ] Checked luggage allowance – and added extra bags if needed
- [ ] Pre-booked airport parking or sorted your lift to the airport
- [ ] Booked or planned the airport lounge / fast track (if you're feeling boujee or travelling with wild children)
- [ ] Notified your bank of international travel (some still flag suspicious transactions)
- [ ] Ordered currency if you need some cash for taxis or snacks on arrival
- [ ] Downloaded offline maps for the area and translation apps
- [ ] Checked the weather at your destination (nearer the trip) – so you don't pack sandals for a rainy week

Part Two
DESTINATION DECISIONS

We embarked on our first multi-destination family trip when Leo was just nine months old. We flew to Santorini as our first stop, staying in three different places across the island. "Why on earth would you want to change hotels?!" everyone asked. And as we dragged our cases and the pram up endless steps in 1,000-degree heat, we were asking ourselves the same thing. But it *was* interesting to see the different holiday experiences we had in the various locations. The island is small, but each town we visited offered a distinctive vibe, and its own unique pros and cons. This was in my "wannabe content creator" era – and the more hotels we could review, the better.

After Santorini, we got the ferry to Mykonos, where we hired a car but stayed in one hotel this time – an undeniably smarter decision. From there, we flew to Paphos in Cyprus, rented another car, and met up with family. That two-week trip was eye-opening yet amazing: three destinations, one baby and only a few mild disasters. It showed us that travelling like this – even with a little one – was totally doable.

"Sure, it's easy with one baby!" I hear you all shouting. And yes, you'd be right. Leo was a dream. I hate calling babies "well-behaved" because babies need what they need. But, if I'm honest, some babies are easier to travel with than others, and Leo was one of the easy ones. Everyone warned us, "It will be different if you have a second!" – the same people had also told us, "You can't travel with kids", but so far, so good; we were managing to. We didn't know it then, but the freedom of that trip would soon feel a million miles away …

It was early 2020. I'd just gone back to work after my maternity leave and the Covid-19 pandemic was kicking off. Returning to work after maternity leave is tough at the best of times, but throw in a global crisis and skeletal staffing, and "tough" became an understatement.

Balancing work with childcare is not easy. I had to be at work for 7:30am and João would leave at 5am for a two-hour commute to Manchester (it was the only option for him at the time). Leo's nursery opened at 7am and was a 40-minute drive from the hospital that I was working at, so the maths wasn't mathin' for my punctual arrival. Every morning, I would be the first in the drop-off queue, waiting to yeet my baby at the nursery staff and then sprint to my car, knowing I was already ten minutes late.

Often Leo would cry, clinging to me, shouting "Ma-ma, Ma-ma" through his little tears. And then I'd cry too, all the way to work, feeling like the worst mum in the world. But what choice did we have? That transition from being home with your baby all day every day, to this, is such an emotionally challenging time.

At the hospital, I'd be taking over from a doctor who'd been on call since 7:30pm the night before. Often, these night-time doctors would be other mums, desperate to get home to their own circus. The later I was, the longer they stayed.

Where there were normally six doctors working, during the pandemic, sometimes there was just one. I worked in general surgery – most juniors had been taken from our wards and were drafted into ICU and medicine, where Covid was having the biggest impact on patient numbers. Routine operating lists were being cancelled to allow for emergency operations to happen. It got to a point where even cancer operations were having to be cancelled, as there just wasn't the capacity to do them and maintain a safe emergency list. How do you choose between operating on a cancer that is currently operable (*but may not be in a month's time*) and doing a life-saving operation for someone? It wasn't easy for the decision-makers at the top. The life- or limb-saving surgery was having to take priority.

Meanwhile, A+E was heaving. I'd often come on shift and have the responsibility of seeing 15 new patients, many of whom had been waiting for hours for a surgical opinion. And that list would continue to grow throughout the day. Many of these patients were really sick. Every patient I saw was angry – about the wait, about the cancelled operations and about their untreated pain. And frontline staff took the brunt of that frustration. Despite the general public standing on their doorsteps and clapping for the NHS, that support was rarely seen in our day-to-day work. And I got it. I knew they weren't receiving the care they would ordinarily get. But that wasn't for a lack of effort; it was a numbers game. As healthcare professionals, we were far outnumbered by patients. I'm a perfectionist, and I love doing the best job possible for my patients. But it wasn't possible anymore. It was a case of doing 15 rushed jobs, and everyone being seen, or doing 5 excellent jobs, knowing the other 10 wouldn't then be seen at all. I love sitting and talking in detail with patients about their new diagnosis, helping them understand it and make the right decisions. But these conversations had become rushed, as more time with one meant less time with the next. We didn't take breaks; at best, I would wolf down a sandwich while sitting at a computer chasing blood and scan results – there just wasn't any time.

Sometimes, the nursery would call and tell me Leo wasn't settling, or had fallen, and I had to explain how I genuinely could not leave work to collect him. And with João two hours away, it was a rubbish situation to be in. I wanted nothing more than to go and scoop up my baby and make him feel safe. But it really was life or death at work, and I frequently had to put that above my baby's needs. We were always the last to pick up Leo. Late again. More apologising. More late fees. What sort of family life was this?

Like many working mums, I'd take Leo from his cot, drive him to nursery, leave him there for 11 hours, pick him up and essentially put him back to bed. I was losing my hair, severely anxious and fantasising about getting Covid just for the time off. I was working endless weekends, covering for colleagues who were off with Covid. It breaks my heart to think of this now, but I often thought about crashing my car on my way to work. A few broken bones would mean I could get a breather. I really was in a bad place mentally. I didn't want to die; I was just at the end of my tether. I needed a break, but couldn't have one without feeling like I was letting the (NHS) team down.

We were surviving, definitely not thriving. Every day we were firefighting just to get to the next.

This went on for two years.

The NHS didn't bounce back – and neither did I. The NHS I remembered from before my maternity leave was gone. Morale was at rock bottom and people were leaving in droves, sometimes for jobs in other countries, sometimes for entirely different careers. I loved my job, but what I'd trained a decade for was now unrecognisable. I'd poured my life into becoming a surgeon ... but what was left of *me*? I was a shell of the bubbly and adventurous person I used to be.

My identity had become being a doctor. How could I leave? What else would I do? A medical degree allows you to be a doctor, and anything else feels impossible. It's like an abusive relationship; I stayed with it for so many years as I didn't think I could live without it. It was good to me every now and again, but most of the time it made me miserable.

It also felt like I was abandoning myself and my dreams. Anyone who has spent their life doing one thing will be able to relate to this. You become that thing that you have worked tirelessly to become. Having grown up on a council estate, and being a woman, I was constantly underestimated. I had proved I was smart, able and deserving through my career. It is incredibly hard to give that away.

The straw that broke the camel's back came one Christmas Day.

I'd just walked onto the ward when the crash alarm went off.

"Surely not first thing on Christmas Day ...?" I thought. I'd hoped someone had pulled the buzzer by mistake. Unfortunately not. A patient I knew well had arrested (meaning her heart had stopped). I ran to the bay and was the first doctor to arrive. A nurse was already doing CPR and someone was running towards us with the crash trolley that had all the equipment and medicine we would need. The patient's husband had just arrived, suited up with some flowers and ready to spend Christmas Day with his wife. She had been in hospital with us for a few weeks, and was known well to our team, with frequent admissions. I had been chatting to her the previous evening about how I'd be back the next day as I was working Christmas Day, and she'd commented how sorry she was that I wouldn't spend the day with my family.

Crash calls are funny things, as it really is the biggest emergency we face, and we are trained so meticulously to deal with them. We are trained to be calm and methodical. It's like a button is pressed and you become this highly efficient robot, asking the right questions while acting and telling other people what they need to get or what they need to do. As more and more people start to arrive, everyone knows what needs to be done and everyone takes on their role. It's like a machine where all the cogs start to assemble and work together perfectly – it really is a beautiful example of how amazing the NHS is and how skilled healthcare staff are. Because for a crash call, there is never a lack of numbers. Everyone drops what they are doing and quite literally runs to help.

Long story short, the lady didn't make it. Once the decision is made to stop, everyone scuttles off to deal with the next crisis that awaits them. The ward quickly becomes quiet. Often the resuscitation attempt will happen in a bay of other patients, all shocked at what they have just witnessed. As I knew the patient well, I took her husband aside with one of the nurses and had to explain the best I could what had happened. During this highly sensitive chat, my pager went off three times. I should have left it outside with another member of staff, but I'd forgotten. A+E were annoyed that patients were building up and I hadn't been to see them yet. I had to end my conversation with the husband as quickly as possible, rushing his questions and leaving him alone on Christmas Day. Then off I went to A+E, where I was met with angry colleagues and patients. The day went on. More shouting. More death. This wasn't an unusual day; this *was* the job. When family and friends would ask, "How was your day?", it would be really hard to answer and condense the emotional rollercoaster I had been on while maintaining confidentiality. I'd usually just reply "good" to avoid discussing it further.

That night, I got home and João and Leo had made me a Christmas card and a cake. They were proud of me. That tiny act of kindness broke down the walls I had built around my emotions that day. I sobbed so hard I couldn't breathe. For the old man who lost his life partner on Christmas morning. For all the times I was shouted at that day. For all the patients I knew I didn't have time to help properly. That day wasn't a one-off. Every day was the same. My stress response was always on high alert. It was exhausting.

Why was I doing this to myself, to my family? I wasn't being paid enough to have *this* be my life. I wasn't respected enough to endure so much mental torture, every single day. I looked at the consultants, the people I was aspiring to be, and they weren't living the dream either.

That night, I drew a line. I had to get out. My family had to come first.

As a completely unrelated creative outlet, I had been posting travel content on TikTok. I love travel. I love making videos. I love helping people find holiday deals. It was nice, it was easy and I enjoyed doing it. I'd gained over 100,000 followers from my little hobby. It was a nice way to completely detach from the eternal stress I was feeling.

I started wondering: could this actually *be* something? I changed my social media handle to @thetravelmum from @jennaraecarr while parked up at work one morning. It felt like a symbolic moment, like the start of something exciting.

Just like in my day job, I faced a lot of negativity on social media. I was often met with critical comments and people being mean. Certain colleagues made fun of what I was doing; people thought I was "cringe". But, by 2022, I'd gained more followers and had landed a few paid brand deals – enough to give me the confidence to make the leap. I quit my job at the hospital and focused fully on building The Travel Mum – as a business, not just as a hobby. People thought I was mad. Who quits medicine to become an "influencer"? But I didn't see it like that – I was building a brand, and the social media videos were just a part of my bigger plan.

Meanwhile, we had been trying for baby number two for some time. We had tests – there was nothing apparent wrong. "Secondary infertility" was thrown into the conversation. We blamed stress, and carried on trying. The last few years had taken a huge toll on my mental health; I was certain things would be better now that I wasn't working at the hospital.

A few months after I quit my job, João did the same. We couldn't live the life we wanted if he was driving to Manchester and back every day. I had a regular brand deal that just about covered our outgoings each month. We had also saved some money to invest into The Travel Mum.

"What's the worst that can happen?!" we thought optimistically. Nothing could be worse than the last few years. And if it all went wrong? At least we'd know we tried and we would go back to our normal jobs. Nothing lost, but a chance for something better.

We leaped into our new travel-blogging lives with another multi-destination trip! Italy: two weeks across Sicily, Naples, the Amalfi Coast and Rome. It was a hit online. Cue the usual negative, "How selfish to drag a child around like that!" comments. But also? Loads of messages from people feeling inspired to do the same.

In this section, we're diving into the destinations that give you the best bang for your buck – from multi-stop road trips and bargain breaks to camping hacks and why a staycation might just be your budget's new best friend. I'm going to share everything I've learned to help you do the same – with minimal chaos, minimal stress and without the judgement.

Let's go!

Chapter Four
DEAL DESTINATIONS

Where you go matters, especially when travelling with a family and on a tight budget. I mean, yes, technically you *could* have a fabulous time anywhere with the right attitude and enough wine, but some places are just easier, cheaper and way more family-friendly.

Picking the right place to visit is the travel equivalent of swiping right. You want the good vibes, the synergy and, ideally, not to be catfished when you arrive. It's not just about who (sorry, *where*) looks pretty – it's about how that destination fits with your family, your finances and the kind of trip you're after. And trust me, I know the power of a good swipe – as you know, I met João after swiping right on him while travelling alone in Portugal. Right place, right time, right swipe. It matters!

It's dangerously easy to get catfished by a "cheap" holiday. You spot a bargain flight, you book it immediately, feel smug for five whole minutes, and then reality hits: the airport's two hours from your hotel, the trains stop running before your flight arrives and even the budget hotels are looking *spenny*. That bargain? Not so bargainy after all, especially when your taxi ends up costing more than *everyone's* flights combined.

Some destinations will make your money go further, your days run smoother and your kids happier (which, let's be honest, is the priority here!). In this chapter, I'm going to break down exactly how to spot those gems: the budget-friendly destinations that deliver big on value, a few of my favourite places that are perfect for family adventures without financial regret and the times of year to go.

CHOOSING A DESTINATION

When picking a destination, it's not just about finding the cheapest flights on comparison sites like Skyscanner and going wherever they take you (although, in fairness, sometimes that *does* work!). It's not even about heading to your favourite package website and listing the prices from low to high. Things are much more complicated when you have kids!

The main things I like to consider include:
- **Affordability once you're there:** Cheap flights to Switzerland are great until you realise a cheese toastie costs £15.
- **Family-friendliness:** Is there something for the kids to do? It doesn't need to be a full-blown theme park – sometimes a simple playground by the beach is enough. Having that one thing they're excited about (aka your go-to parenting threat) can make your day *so* much smoother. "If you don't stop that, we're not going to the playground!" may or may not have left my mouth on one or two occasions … Some places "get" kids and others definitely don't. For younger kids, think are there playgrounds? Family rooms? Baby changing? With older kids, look out for ice cream parlours, water sports and arcades – it can all make or break a trip.
- **Travel time:** How tolerant are your kids when it comes to travel? Consider the flight time plus the transfer time to the hotel on the other side. After a long flight with young kids, you might want to choose a destination that isn't too far from the airport.

So, what makes a destination budget-friendly? You're looking for:
- **Free or cheap things to do:** Think beaches, nature trails, public parks, scenic walks, free museums or cultural sites. Flesh out the activity schedule with as many of these as possible.
- **Affordable food options:** Street food, casual local restaurants, family-run cafés or supermarkets where you can grab picnic bits and snacks without breaking the bank are a must.

- **Cheap and easy public transport:** Trams, buses, metro systems or even bike hire that make getting around a breeze *without* needing pricey taxis or car hire make all the difference to your budget. Cities that are close to the airport with cheap public transport are great options. Porto, Copenhagen and Palma de Mallorca are some of our European faves for this.
- **Family discounts and city passes:** Multi-attraction cards that cover museums, transport or even meals are great for squeezing the most out of a short trip. It goes without saying, but these are only good value if you actually want to do the activities included. We have fallen into the trap of spending more on a pass than the one activity we actually wanted to do! Forcing a reluctant young child to visit a textile museum, just because it's included in the pass, maybe isn't the best way to spend your time.
- **Reasonably priced accommodation:** Hotels, guesthouses or apartments that offer kitchens (think DIY breakfast) or include meals and extras like free parking or airport transfers are all good options.
- **Budget airlines or trains:** Getting there without spending a fortune is half the battle. If the destination is catered to by a convenient and cheap airline or train route, it's going to really help keep the trip cheap. Bonus points if the airport or station isn't miles from civilisation.
- **A favourable exchange rate:** Your money goes further in places where the cost of living is lower than at home and the exchange rate is good – getting more holiday for your hard-earned cash is always a win.
- **Off-season perks:** Outside of peak season, there are cheaper prices, fewer crowds and accommodation deals galore – and if the weather plays nice, it's a total win. My husband's from the Algarve, and we *always* visit outside peak summer. It's cooler for the kids and much less crowded – a great option for May and October half terms (in the UK).

HIDDEN GEM DESTINATIONS FOR FAMILIES

Why elbow your way through the selfie-stick jungle of Venice when you could be drifting down the canals of Annecy, France – a beautiful alpine town with canals, colourful buildings and zero gondola traffic jams. Travelling with kids doesn't mean you have to follow the crowd. In fact, some of the best family adventures happen in places that haven't been completely taken over by cruise ship hordes and overpriced gelato.

Below are some underrated destinations you may not have thought of that are packed with charm, adventure and affordability.

Europe
- **Slovenia:** Lake Bled is straight out of a fairy tale – a little church on an island, a castle perched on a cliff and more open space than your kids will know what to do with. If your family loves the outdoors, this place is a dream: think lakeside walks, paddleboarding and picnics with a view. Slovenia's also refreshingly compact, so you can pack in mountains, lakes and even underground caves without spending half your holiday stuck in transit.
- **Bosnia and Herzegovina:** Forget crowded Dubrovnik. Bosnia offers dramatic waterfalls (look up Kravica Falls), Ottoman-style towns like Mostar and breathtaking mountain scenery.
- **Northern Spain:** Skip the tourist-heavy south and head north for San Sebastián's family-friendly beaches, world-famous pintxos (a type of Basque-style tapas) and lush countryside. The Basque Country and Asturias are incredible.
- **Albania:** This was once Europe's best-kept secret for sun-seekers – until social media blew its cover. Expect turquoise waters, crumbling castle ruins and beachside seafood that won't rinse your bank account. Head to the Albanian Riviera for laid-back beach vibes or swing by Berat for cobbled streets and a hit of history.
- **Bulgaria:** The Black Sea coast is dotted with sandy beaches and affordable family resorts. Places like Sozopol and Nessebar offer

history and sunshine without the price tag of Greece or Italy. Bansko is a great option if you're looking for a budget-friendly ski trip.
- **Montenegro:** The Bay of Kotor gives you fjord-style views, medieval towns and warm waters – perfect for a low-key family escape with dramatic backdrops for your Insta snaps.
- **The Azores, Portugal:** An archipelago in the middle of the Atlantic where you can go whale watching, hike volcanoes and soak in hot springs. Think Hawaiian vibes without breaking the bank. It's nature-focused, peaceful and still blissfully tourist-light.

Beyond Europe
- **Sri Lanka:** This is a brilliant choice for adventurous families. Safari in Yala National Park, explore ancient cities like Sigiriya, chill on the beaches of Mirissa and hop on one of the world's most scenic train journeys from Ella to Kandy. Bonus: the locals absolutely adore children.
- **Malaysia:** With a brilliant mix of cultures, food and landscapes, Malaysia is one of my top recommendations. The capital, Kuala Lumpur, is super easy to navigate, and you've got lush jungles in Langkawi, tea plantations in the Cameron Highlands and orangutans in Borneo if you're up for the adventure. The Perhentian islands are off the beaten trail and have stunning beaches.
- **South Africa:** With sun-soaked beaches, incredible wildlife and rich culture, South Africa has it all. Cape Town is bursting with family-friendly adventures, from spotting the famous penguins at Boulders Beach to taking the cable car up Table Mountain. You can even tick a safari off your bucket list and, of course, squeeze in a little wine tasting while you're there (because holidays aren't *just* about the kids!).
- **Taiwan:** A super safe and surprisingly affordable destination, Taiwan allows you to explore night markets, visit quirky

museums and soak in hot springs. The public transport is fab and locals are really welcoming to families.
- **Uruguay:** Often overlooked in favour of Argentina or Brazil, Uruguay offers laid-back beach towns like Punta del Diablo, horse riding in the countryside and the charming capital of Montevideo – without the chaos of bigger tourist hotspots.
- **Georgia (the country, not the US state):** Nestled between Europe and Asia, Georgia offers incredible mountain scenery, ancient monasteries, warm hospitality and delicious food. It's great for families looking for something a bit different but is still very safe and affordable.

TOP TIP
Don't overlook staycations.
There's a whole chapter dedicated to this (*Chapter Six, p122*), but staycations are especially good if you're struggling to find the budget for a trip abroad.

SEASONAL TRAVEL TIPS

Timing is everything. Certain times of year mean better deals, fewer crowds and weather that won't have you hiding in a supermarket air-con aisle. A word of warning though: some destinations go full-on *ghost town* outside of peak season. That dreamy beach break you just grabbed for peanuts? It might look like a Mediterranean postcard online, but rock up in March and you could be greeted by closed shutters, sideways rain and tumbleweed blowing down the promenade. Personally, I love the eerie calm of an off-season seaside town – no crowds, no queues, no one trying to sell you a selfie stick – but I fully accept I might be alone in that.

A lot of these places are built *purely* for tourists, which means when the tourists leave, so does everything else. Restaurants? Shut. Bars? Dark. Shops? Long gone. Sure, the hotels stay open and the prices drop so low they practically pay *you* to stay, but don't get duped by a too-good-to-be-true all-inclusive unless you've checked what's going on during that period of the year.

That said, if your idea of bliss is quiet beaches, long walks and eating your body weight in buffet food, then off-season all-inclusive might just be your golden ticket: less buzz, more bargains – and the kids won't care as long as they've got sandcastles to build and snacks to demolish. After all, at their core, kids are simple. Give them a spade to dig in the sand, a climbing frame to conquer, a ball to chase – or even just your undivided attention – and they'll be in their element. They don't need flashy, expensive attractions to have the time of their lives. We have visited tons of theme parks and, most of the time, Leo's favourite part will be the playground or the time he spent drawing what he did that day once we were home.

Naturally, the sweet spot varies by destination, but here's a month-by-month guide to where your money can stretch further – while keeping your sanity intact:

January

Got the post-Christmas blues? Escape them.
- **Poland:** Hit the slopes in Zakopane for a family ski holiday that is easy on the wallet. As an added bonus, they keep their Christmas decs up into February for a prolonged festive period! We recently shared a chalet here with some friends and enjoyed a lovely, budget-friendly ski trip. It's also perfect for beginners and families who want to try skiing without the huge price tag.
- **Canary Islands:** Sunshine, beaches and toddler-friendly temps – what more could you want? Our favourite island is Lanzarote, and we particularly love Playa Blanca in the south as it is less windy than some of the towns on the east coast.
- **Egypt:** With warm weather, ancient wonders and hotel deals galore, I would highly recommend Hurghada or Sharm el-Sheikh. The hotels here tend to be brilliant for kids with tons of activities.

February
Treat your partner to a romantic getaway (with the kids, of course!).
- **Portugal:** Cities like Lisbon or Porto are mild, uncrowded and very walkable.
- **Dubai:** At this time of year, it's still warm but not scorching, and prices dip after New Year.
- **Lapland:** Perfect for those wanting to squeeze in a snowy escape before the season ends – and Santa is there all year round, so why not visit him when he is less busy?!

March
Spring sunshine and no queues – what's not to love?
- **Rome** or **Barcelona:** Enjoy iconic sights without melting or queueing for hours.
- **Seville:** With early spring warmth and blooming orange trees, this is one of my favourite cities, but it gets way too hot in the summer.
- **The Algarve:** This is a fave for us with its cheap flights, stunning beaches and coastal walks. Pack trousers and a T-shirt, plan a picnic on the beach and soak in that warm (but not too warm) sun.

April
Get away for the Easter school holidays.
- **Cyprus:** This is a great shoulder season option, especially Paphos.
- **Madeira:** Ideal for hiking families and nature lovers, the island is known for its beautiful scenery and family-friendly atmosphere.
- **Germany:** Plan a road trip in the Black Forest region and visit Europa-Park and Rulantica water park.

May
This is one of the best months for travel (in my opinion).
- **Greece:** Warm enough to swim, cool enough to sleep – the perfect balance for a family getaway. Don't just stick to the islands; the Halkidiki peninsula and Peloponnese coast are home to some fantastic, budget-friendly resorts that are great for families.

- **Turkey:** Resorts along the Antalya coast are incredibly family-friendly and still affordable before the summer rush.
- **Sicily:** Home to great weather, low crowds and family-friendly beaches. Consider planning this one as a DIY trip as opposed to a package – it's often much cheaper this way.

June
The sun's out, and the prices are still reasonable (just!).
- **Croatia:** Beat the summer madness and enjoy places like Zadar, Split or the islands while they're still peaceful.
- **Montenegro:** Think fjords, beaches and budget-friendly beauty.
- **Albania:** A fantastic value option, some beach resorts on the Albanian Riviera (mainly Ksamil) can get very crowded in the peak months. Early June is a great time to visit.

July
I know it's peak season, but there are still hacks.
- **Poland:** Fly to Gdańsk and visit the beaches on the Baltic coast. Perfect if, like me, you hate the intense heat in southern Europe.
- **Northern Spain:** Cooler than the south and way less touristy, this is a great place for a camper van road trip (*p111*)!
- **Slovenia:** Great for outdoorsy families – enjoy the lakes, hikes and fresh air all round.

August
Yes, it's pricey, but yes, you can still beat the system.
- **Bulgaria:** Black Sea resorts are much cheaper than their Mediterranean neighbours.
- **Hungary:** Lake Balaton is a summer favourite with locals and a hit with families.
- **Abu Dhabi:** I know this is an unexpected recommendation for August, but it's relatively cheap due to being very hot. There are lots of indoor attractions and the country is set up for the heat, so August is a good time to visit for some bargain luxury.

September

This is one of the golden months for bargain-hunters.
- **Florida:** Once US schools are back, prices drop dramatically. Florida is a popular family destination for a reason! Visit some of the best theme parks in the world, spot alligators from an airboat ride on the Everglades, snorkel alongside manatees or relax at Clearwater Beach (which has the whitest sand I've ever seen!).
- **Malta:** It's still hot and still beautiful at this time of year, and flights are often great value.
- **Southern Italy:** The weather's gorgeous and the crowds have gone home – win-win.

SHOULDER SEASONS = SMART SEASONS

Travel just before or after peak times (known as the shoulder season). You still get good weather, the prices are cheaper and fewer people will be ruining your photos. Hotels and hosts are often extra-friendly when they're not overwhelmed, which is an added bonus. We've had more upgrades and unexpected perks during shoulder season than at any other time. So, why not plan your big family holiday in the school holidays that happen before or after the summer? You'll get more for your money, and can enjoy the summer months at home.

October
October is a very popular time to travel, especially with half term at the end of the month (in the UK), but there are still deals to be had.
- **Cyprus:** There will still be plenty of sunshine for days at the beach. Note that it can be pricey if you are booking last minute for the half term.
- **Morocco:** Great for sunshine and souks without the searing heat. You can find some absolutely brilliant prices in October. Agadir is a great beach resort for families.
- **Canary Islands:** Great if you are looking for reliable sunshine and lots of family-friendly resorts.

November
This month offers a sneaky travel window if you can swing it.
- **The Gambia:** It has a short-ish flight time from the UK, hot weather and a real cultural experience.
- **Thailand:** The rainy season ends, but prices are still low. With beautiful beaches, lush forests, bustling cities and affordable accommodation, this is a great option for an adventurous family.
- **Cape Verde:** Hot, dry and just six hours from the UK, this is a great option for finding hot weather without a long-haul flight.

December
Festive travel doesn't have to cost a fortune. Try to avoid the Christmas school holidays if you can.
- **Tenerife:** Christmas on the beach? Yes please. Tenerife has a very mild winter and, as an all-year-round destination, there is lots to see and do.
- **Czech Republic:** Think cosy Christmas markets in Prague without the Vienna prices. Pick up some quirky Christmas gifts for the family and take the kids to visit Santa.
- **Sri Lanka:** If you're looking for a big trip, this is the perfect time to explore both the beaches and hill country. There'll be warm, sunny days with very little rain.

TOP TIP
Always check school term dates in your area *and* the local area you're visiting.
Some destinations spike in price when local holidays hit, even if it's not school holidays in the UK.

WEEKEND AND CITY BREAKS

You don't need a two-week escape to make epic memories. A cheeky weekend away can work wonders for your sanity *and* your annual leave. City breaks get a bad rap when it comes to kids, but, trust me, they can be surprisingly family-friendly. And who says beach holidays have to be long and pricey? A long weekend on a beautiful island might be the perfect sweet spot between escapism and budget.

Here are my top tips for weekend trips:
- **Use budget airlines tactically:** Do you really need to book seats in advance? Probably not.
- **Maximise your time away:** Book the earliest outbound and latest return flights you can stomach. Yes, it means brutal alarms and possibly feeding kids crisps for breakfast at the airport, but it gives you nearly an *extra day* of exploring.
- **Pack light:** This means you avoid luggage charges – and stress *(see p48 for my tips on packing light)*.
- **Roll your kids' clothes into Ziplock bags by outfit (one per day):** Saves faffing and prevents the "Mum, I can't find my socks!" meltdown in a shoebox-sized hotel room.
- **Stay central:** You can then walk everywhere – perfect when you're limited for time.
- **Look out for affordable lunchtime menus:** Many cities offer three courses for the price of one sad Pret sandwich back home. Fill up then, and you can coast on a cheap snack dinner later.
- **Check for free things to do:** These include children's museums, parks and local events.

- **Build in "micro-activities" between sights:** Think carousel rides, browsing toy shops and even chasing pigeons in a town square. It costs pennies, buys you sanity and avoids full-scale mutiny.
- **Book apartment-style accommodation:** This gifts you cheap DIY breakfasts and space for tantrums.

And if you're wondering how to entertain kids on a city break:
- Look for big parks and interactive museums.
- Try geocaching! (Google it if you haven't heard of it.)
- Teach the kids some interesting age-appropriate facts about the place you're visiting. We recently went to Venice and Leo loved learning about how the city was built on water.
- Look for local theme parks and zoos *(see p134 for my tips on visiting theme parks on a budget)*.
- Older kids may enjoy looking for Instagrammable spots.
- Try alternative transport methods like Segways or electric scooters.
- Try some sporty activities like rock climbing or ice skating.

TOP TIP
Search for "playgrounds" near your accommodation.
Open your maps app, "star" a few playgrounds in advance and have them ready. When everyone's melting down mid-sightseeing, whip out a hidden gem play area like the hero you are. Find a bench in the shade, get some ice cream and let the kids run wild for half an hour.

Being on a budget doesn't mean boring holidays. With a little research and clever planning, you can have unique, exciting and Instagram-worthy (if that's your thing) adventures. Now, go find your next deal destination!

Great destinations deserve great adventures – and sometimes the best way to see it all is by hitting the open road with a great playlist and a boot full of snacks. In the next chapter, we'll explore the joys (and chaos) of family road trips.

DESTINATION DUPES

Want the vibe without the price tag?

INSTEAD OF ...	TRY ...	WHY ...
Amsterdam, Netherlands	**Ghent or Utrecht**	Canals and bikes galore, but with lower prices and fewer tourists.
Bali, Indonesia	**Lombok, Indonesia**	Beautiful beaches, waterfalls and surf – minus the crowds and Insta tax.
Barcelona, Spain	**Valencia, Spain**	Beach city vibes, Gaudí-esque architecture and fewer stag dos.
Cinque Terre, Italy	**Puglia's seaside towns, Italy**	Clifftop villages and sea views – without needing to remortgage.
Croatia	**Bosnia and Herzegovina**	Gorgeous coastline (hello, Neum!), charming old towns and very budget-friendly.
Dubai	**Abu Dhabi**	Similar luxury, beaches and theme parks, but often with cheaper hotels and fewer crowds.
Iceland	**The Azores**	Volcanoes, hot springs and epic nature – but cheaper flights and food.
Lake Como, Italy	**Lake Maggiore, Italy**	The same Italian lake charm, with prettier price tags and fewer influencers.
Norway fjords	**Georgia (the country)**	Epic mountains and lakes with a side of khachapuri (a traditional Georgian dish of cheese-filled bread) and no £9 pints.

INSTEAD OF ...	TRY ...	WHY ...
Paris, France	Lyon or Strasbourg, France	French charm, riverside cafés and architecture without the inflated prices.
Santorini, Greece	Naxos or Milos, Greece	Whitewashed villages, yummy gyros and sunsets, but half the price.
Seychelles	Zanzibar	White-sand beaches and tropical vibes – for a more down-to-earth cost.
St. Lucia	Dominican Republic	Tropical paradise, snorkelling and turquoise seas – on a much lower budget.
Swiss Alps	Julian Alps, Slovenia	Jaw-dropping mountains, lakes and hiking, but less spenny.
The Maldives resorts	The Maldives local islands	Turquoise waters, gorgeous beaches and perfect snorkelling without the luxury price tag.
Tokyo, Japan	Taipei, Taiwan	Neon lights, temples and amazing food – and far gentler on your bank account.
Tuscany, Italy	Douro Valley, Portugal	Vineyards, rolling hills and scenic towns – with better value wine tastings.
Venice, Italy	Aveiro, Portugal	Cute canals and colourful boats – without the overpriced gondola guilt.

Chapter Five
THE ART OF THE FAMILY ROAD TRIP (WITHOUT LOSING YOUR SANITY)

We *love* a road trip. Whether we're in our own car, behind the wheel of a hire car or embracing the freedom of a camper van, there's something very exciting about hitting the road with minimal plans. Being able to see and explore multiple destinations in one trip? Right up our street – literally.

We're the kind of people who *try* to book relaxing holidays by the pool, but, five minutes in, we're googling waterfalls, hidden beaches or "cool things to do near here". We just love an adventure and have a serious case of location FOMO (fear of missing out!).

So, picture this: you're cruising down a scenic road, your favourite playlist on, the kids not arguing for once and the open road ahead looking beautiful and promising adventure. Fancy stopping at the nearby theme park for a thrilling day of rides? Do it! Everyone tired and in need of some chill? Find a campsite or beach and relax for the day. The world is your oyster. I can't promise it'll always be this serene, but when it works, it works.

Road trips and multi-destination travel are total game changers for families. Yet, for whatever reason, a lot of families shudder at the thought. But think about it: you're not stuck in one spot, you can flex the plan as you go and, if you play your cards right, you can keep things affordable *and* exciting. Whether you're hiring a car, hopping between cities by train or going full #VanLife, this chapter's here to help you do it all – without needing a second mortgage (or a therapist).

WHY ROAD TRIPS ARE PERFECT FOR FAMILIES

Let's start with the obvious benefit: flexibility. Kids want snacks at random times, someone needs a wee every 27 minutes and you'll probably spot at least one unexpected castle/zoo/funfair on your route that demands a spontaneous detour. Road trips let you run on *your* schedule. They can be as laid back or as structured as you like. If your family are early risers, set off for the day's events at 6am; there's nothing to stop you. If you all like a lie-in, casually set off at lunchtime. Planned to set off at 6am but three tantrums and a last-minute poosplosion have slowed you down? It's not a problem.

When you are exploring places through planned excursions or by public transport, you are a lot more restricted with timings, which can be really stressful as a family with young kids. If your expensive excursion needs you all to meet in Reception at 7am, but the kids have decided they don't want to wake up … Good luck!

Then there's the bonding. There's something special about singing along to cheesy music and your fave Disney tracks, playing silly games like I spy and having that "We're all in this together" mentality (cue *High School Musical* soundtrack). It's the stuff core memories are made of. Both my husband and I did a lot of road trips with our families growing up, and we've always wanted our kids to have similar happy memories.

And it's not just practical – it's unique. A multi-stop journey can turn a simple holiday into an epic family adventure. One day, you're swimming in lakes; the next, you're enjoying a theme park; the next, you're eating gelato on a cobbled street. Variety is the spice of road tripping.

PLANNING A ROAD TRIP

Planning a road trip can feel overwhelming at first, especially with kids, but I promise it's much simpler than it seems.

Car versus camper van hire
Both car and camper van hire have their perks. Both options could be the cheaper option, depending on accommodation costs and camper rules in your chosen destination, so let's get into the details so you can decide which is right for you.

Car travel
If you're planning to travel by car, you will need to book accommodation along your route (or bring a tent to cut costs!). Staying in guesthouses, roadside hotels, hostels and apartment rentals can be cheaper than booking fancy hotels. You will need to consider the price of car hire plus all of your nightly accommodation when working out which will be the best value. It will likely be cheaper to book your accommodation in advance, meaning you need to have a bit of a plan, which could be restricting for those wanting that full wild and free experience. Travelling with a car can be easier if you want to visit a lot of cities – parking spaces large enough for camper vans can be limited (but never impossible to find).

Camper van travel
Travelling in a camper van is a fun and unique way to get around as a family. You can often arrive with zero plan and make it up as you go along – something we really enjoy doing. With your kitchen, bed, toilet and transport all in one, it can be a great value way to travel. There are a few things to consider with a camper van holiday, such as:
- **Is wild camping allowed where you are going?** Some countries will allow you to park up for the night anywhere, meaning minimal additional costs and beautiful woodland/beachside spots. Some countries will require you to book campsites for the night, which come with a cost. We have paid €5 for the night, all the way up to €80, depending on facilities and availability in the area. *(See the box on p112 for more on this.)*

- **How big are you willing to go?** Bigger isn't always better, especially when driving on narrow country roads (with zero experience driving anything bigger than your Vauxhall Corsa).
- **How many belted seats does it have?** And remember to consider whether your car seats will fit.
- **Do you need a toilet for the night-times?** This is important to consider when wild camping and also with young children (or mums with weak bladders). Campsites will have a toilet block, but running out in the cold during the night can be inconvenient.
- **What are the sleeping arrangements?** Just because it *technically* sleeps the right number of people, consider whether you will all be comfortable doing that for the length of your trip.

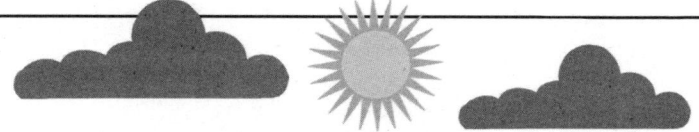

WILD CAMPING

Some countries – especially in Europe – are totally cool with wild camping, thanks to something called "right to roam" or "everyman's right" (basically, nature is for sharing). It usually comes with a bit of common sense: don't be a nuisance, and leave the place looking like you were never there. Being able to camp without paying for a campsite can massively cut costs.

I have listed below some places where it is OK to wild camp (at the time of writing).

Legal (with responsible rules):
- **Scotland:** Thanks to the Land Reform Act, you can wild camp (except in restricted areas like Loch Lomond). Just be respectful and follow the Scottish Outdoor Access Code. Wild camping is not generally permitted in England, Wales or Northern Ireland.

- **Norway:** "Allemannsretten" (everyman's right) means you can camp freely on uncultivated land, as long as you're 150 metres from houses and stay no more than two nights in one spot.
- **Sweden:** "Allemansrätten" gives similar rights as Norway to roam and camp, with the same general rules around distance and respect.
- **Finland:** Finland also embraces everyman's right. Wild camping is allowed on public land, including forests and lakesides. Fires may be restricted, so check local advice.
- **Estonia:** Wild camping is allowed in most places, including national parks, as long as you follow signage and keep it tidy.

Tolerated (use common sense):
- **Iceland:** Was legal, but now restricted due to tourism. You can wild camp in some rural areas (not near homes or on cultivated land), but national parks are usually off-limits.
- **Latvia and Lithuania:** Generally accepted in nature areas, including forests and beaches, as long as it's not marked as private.
- **Austria:** Not strictly legal, but often tolerated in remote alpine areas. Some federal states have stricter rules.
- **Spain:** It's complicated. Wild camping is technically illegal, but often tolerated in remote, non-touristy areas. Each region has different rules, so do your research. We have camped in a few wooded areas in Andalucia.
- **Portugal:** Previously tolerated, but rules are stricter now. Camper vans can use marked "áreas de serviço" for cheap or free, which are plentiful and a safer bet than risking a fine.
- **France:** Technically allowed – *if* you've got the landowner's blessing. So, unless you've charmed a French farmer or made besties with a vineyard owner, you'll need to ask first. Oh, and heads up: camping on the coast, in protected nature spots or near fancy historic sites is a big non-non. Stick to the rules, pitch discreetly and you should be fine.

Don't fancy driving?

I appreciate not everyone can (or wants to) drive on holiday, but that doesn't make road trips out of reach. Europe's rail systems are fab for family travel. Interrail passes can be amazing value, especially with younger children, who often travel for free. The trains become part of the adventure – plus, nobody has to drive (hello, afternoon aperitif) and you can play Uno without worrying about potholes ruining the fun. If you decide to travel by train with kids, try to book seats at a table (built-in colouring station!) or in family carriages when available. Sitting near the doors = noisy, draughty and more foot traffic.

Budgeting on the road

Here are my top tips for keeping the costs down when planning a family road trip:

- **Make the most of apps:** Use apps like PetrolPrices (UK) or GasBuddy (USA) to find the cheapest fuel nearby, and apps like park4night are great for finding free parking spaces for camper vans.
- **Don't forget about tolls:** These can really mug you off mid-road trip. Check if your map app has a "no tolls" option when setting the route. Sometimes it adds a quick detour, sometimes it's a three-hour magical mystery tour no one asked for. Work out if the savings justify the additional time in the car.
- **Factor in campsite or accommodation fees:** And remember: free wild camping is only legal in some places – see the list on p112.
- **Book train travel in advance:** The differences in price can be *wild*. Check if seat reservations are needed. Bullet trains in Japan, for example, need a seat reservation to guarantee that you can sit together. (You have the option to sit in the "non-reserved car" without a seat reservation, but this could mean everyone sitting separately.) Make sure you know the rules for where you are travelling.
- **Make the most of picnic lunches, street food and supermarket raids:** This will save you a fortune. Look out for things like

"menú del día", "menu du jour" or kids' specials in Europe – €10 for three courses beats €10 for one sad burger.
- **Track your spending on the go:** Keep a travel wallet or app to keep track of your outgoings while you're on the move.
- **Avoid car seat rental costs:** Take your own car seats as daily rental prices can really add up. (Rental seats aren't always the best quality either – *see box below*.)

SAFETY CONSIDERATIONS

It's not the fun stuff, but it's *vital*.

- **Give your car/van a quick "MOT":** Always check tyre pressure, water and oil before setting off.

- **Have an emergency kit:** Include a warning triangle, torch, spare phone charger and first aid kit in the boot. Also check any specific requirements in the country you're visiting.

- **Take your own car seats:** If you're hiring a car abroad, don't assume the child seat will be decent. Half the time they look like they've survived a war. Either bring your own or double-check reviews before you go.

- **Travel insurance is a must:** Always. Even if it's just for a weekend trip.

- **Check your breakdown cover:** When hiring a camper van, make sure you've got roadside assistance that actually covers camper vans. There's nothing worse than discovering your policy only covers "cars under 3.5 tonnes" while you're stuck in the Alps.

PLAN THE ROUTE (BUT KEEP IT CHILL)

My biggest tip when planning a road trip with kids is to choose scenic but sensible routes. No one wants a six-hour detour just to see "the biggest corn maze in Western Europe". We personally try to keep the driving on travel days under 1.5 hours (3 hours max). I appreciate this is easier in Europe where things are much closer together. Sometimes, driving much further is needed, but we will break it up with an attraction or opportunity to stretch everyone's legs.

Make sure you build in time for proper rest days – your future self will thank you. It is easy to get overexcited when planning this type of trip as you want to see *everything*, but moving every morning gets exhausting, for you and the kids. Having some days when you have zero plans is essential. You might all be buzzing and energetic, in which case go for it and do something exciting! But if you need some time to just lie in, take the kids to the campsite shop and do very little, be sure to build in the time for it. It will make the trip much more enjoyable.

> **TOP TIP**
> **Get the kids involved with the plan.**
> Show them pictures and let them help pick a stop or even vote on lunch spots. With your rest days, ask them, "Do you want to hang around here today or go to one of these places?" Big kids will love getting involved with navigation too. I find that if kids feel included, they are much less likely to whinge!

Staying flexible

If you've booked accommodation or campsites for every night in advance, you are somewhat stuck to that schedule. But, for us, one of the best bits of road tripping is the spontaneity it allows. Found a beach you love? Stay longer. Discovered that the "eco-hostel" you were keen to stay in smells like feet? Move on. *But* – being flexible only really works if it's not high season, and if you've left gaps in your bookings.

A flexible itinerary works best when you've got a bit of wiggle room, you don't have your heart set on specific accommodation/

campsites and you have a plan B. We will often book our first night so we have somewhere to head to on arrival. We will maybe book a night or two in the middle at somewhere we know will book up in advance. But we always leave days free in between so we can decide as we go. Sometimes, the best finds happen unexpectedly, or you get some local advice that adds a new destination to your list. Having some flexibility to go with the flow is what makes these trips exciting for us. If you're travelling during peak times, especially in popular destinations, *some* pre-booking is wise, especially for family-friendly spots that fill up fast.

Entertainment for the road

This is key to survival when road tripping with kids. You need to be ready to throw something at them the second you sense boredom creeping in. It doesn't have to be anything too complex and will obviously vary with age. Some of our faves include:

- **Games:** There are so many on-the-road games you can play as a family to keep kids entertained – think I spy, Road Trip Bingo, "Would You Rather?", each pick a colour and then compete to find the most cars, 20 questions to guess my animal … And not forgetting my favourite one: "Who can stay quiet the longest?" The winner gets a prize. Make sure you've got a deck of cards or mini board games for downtime at your accommodation too.
- **Storytelling:** With little kids, start a silly story ("Once upon a time, a llama climbed a tree …") and let each person add a line. It often descends into nonsense so funny it distracts even the grumpiest child.
- **Devices:** Don't forget to pack headphones (and portable chargers!) – these are your best friend for some peace and quiet.
- **Kid-friendly audiobooks:** Think Roald Dahl or *Harry Potter*. Short, funny podcasts can also be absolute game changers on a long journey. They come with less parent guilt than everyone disappearing into screens.

- **A road trip playlist:** Let everyone pick a few songs. Alongside "Raining Tacos", "Steve's Lava Chicken" is another favourite of ours at the moment (I apologise in advance).
- **Swap places if you can:** If you've got more than one adult, swap who sits in the back every few hours. Sometimes just having "Mum in the backseat" is enough novelty to reset moods.

REAL TALK: OUR ROAD TRIP WINS AND FAILS

We have a lot of experience with this type of family travel, from train-hopping through Japan, camper-vanning in Spain to hiring a car and exploring Lapland. We try to make them easy to replicate, and write about them on our website blog if you want to know the details. Each trip has had its own set of dramas, but we always try to remember that the things that don't go to plan are the things we will look back on and laugh about with the kids.

We once picked up a camper van for our very first camper van adventure, absolutely buzzing with excitement. We were ready to be wild, free and to become that smug van life family. First stop? The supermarket – because nothing says "off-grid living" like a pre-packed supermarket picnic. We headed straight to the beach, feeling like pro travel influencers ... until reality hit: wild camping wasn't allowed and we had *no idea* where we were sleeping that night.

By the time we'd finished our seaside sandwiches, it was pitch black and we started checking out local campsites online. The first one? Full. The second? Also full. The third? You guessed it – fully booked.

Cue the chaos, bickering and desperate phone calls to anywhere with a patch of grass and a working toilet. Eventually, somewhere said yes – hallelujah. We parked up, dragged out our little table and chairs, and cracked open a much-needed beer. Finally, we were living the dream. Until, the heavens opened. I'm talking *biblical* rain, sideways wind, our awning doing a dramatic flappy dance and my last nerve fluttering off into the storm.

Later that night, I attempted a shower in the coffin-sized van bathroom and was warned by a sign on the wall – very seriously – not to wet said walls. As the shower curtain stuck to places it had no business being, I sat down on the loo, naked and emotional, wondering how the hell we had two more weeks of this. But here's the twist: it ended up being one of the best trips we've *ever* taken. We laughed (eventually), we learned (a lot) and we came out of it stronger (and smellier).

Moral of the story? A bad start doesn't mean a bad trip – sometimes it just makes the best stories. Also, basically all of our disasters have come from being underprepared. We live and learn – we've made the mistakes so you don't have to!

Some of our favourite routes we have personally done as a family and would highly recommend include:

- **Croatia:** Zadar–Plitvice–Split–Dubrovnik by car
- **England:** Brighton–Dorset–Devon–Cornwall by car
- **Germany:** Stuttgart–Baden Baden–Freudenstadt–Strasbourg (France)–Colmar (France)–Europa-Park (theme park in Germany) by camper van
- **Italy:** Milan–Lake Como or Lake Garda–Verona–Venice by car or train; or Naples–Pompeii–Sorrento–Amalfi Coast by train
- **Japan:** Tokyo–Kyoto–Osaka–Kobe–Hiroshima–Kanazawa by train
- **Lapland:** Rovaniemi–Levi–Inari by car
- **Portugal:** Faro–Albufeira–Portimão–Lagos–Sagres by camper van
- **Spain:** Malaga–Nerja–Granada–Cordoba–Seville–Ronda–Cadiz–Estepona by camper van

Road trips and multi-destination travel give you the power to explore more, spend less and create unforgettable epic family memories. It might not always be smooth sailing (or driving), but with a bit of planning and a sense of humour it can be absolute magic.

Of course, you don't always need to cross borders or clock up miles to have an unforgettable trip. In the next chapter, we'll explore the humble staycation – proof that amazing family memories can be made without even leaving the country.

ROAD TRIP PACKING ESSENTIALS

Here's your road trip kit:

- [ ] Travel docs and insurance
- [ ] Car seats to save money on renting them
- [ ] A car phone holder if you plan to use your phone for navigation
- [ ] Offline maps (just in case!)
- [ ] Emergency kit for the car
- [ ] First aid kit
- [ ] Motion sickness tablets or bands and sick bags
- [ ] Snacks
- [ ] A cool bag for impromptu picnic lunches and a picnic blanket (for lunch stops / naps in a field)
- [ ] Reusable cutlery and cups (for when you've had enough of crumb-covered laps)
- [ ] Reusable water bottles
- [ ] Neck pillows and blankets
- [ ] Sunshades for the car/train windows
- [ ] Chargers, *all* the cables and a power bank or three

- ☐ A day bag with spare clothes, especially for little ones who like to surprise you with mud, ice cream ... or worse

- ☐ Biodegradable wet wipes (you can never have too many wet wipes) and hand sanitiser

- ☐ A roll of bin bags – trust me, you'll thank me later

- ☐ An entertainment bag (containing cards, games and books) plus a "surprise bag" of new cheap toys/stickers/books to hand out mid-meltdown

- ☐ Small change for tolls/toilets

- ☐ Sunglasses and SPF

- ☐ A travel potty or toilet training kit (if relevant – absolute lifesaver)

- ☐ Spotify/playlist downloaded

- ☐ Notepad and pens (for doodles, games or even emergency peacekeeping treaties)

Chapter Six
STAYCATION SAVVY

A few years ago, I finally realised that *being on holiday is a mindset*. You don't need to be halfway across the world, sipping something coconut-based, to feel like you've escaped real life. And being halfway across the world doesn't guarantee anything; I've sat on a paradise beach feeling more stressed than I did camping in a damp field in Somerset.

Physically removing yourself from your everyday life definitely *helps*, but it's not essential. If your budget isn't quite stretching to a trip abroad, that doesn't mean you can't make incredible memories with your family. You just need to shift your perspective – and maybe pack a flask.

Scotland, for example, is on *countless* global travel wish lists. American folks are flying over ten hours to visit places that are a few hours' drive from me. And there I am, jetting in the opposite direction to explore the very place they just escaped. The irony? I've barely scratched the surface of the beauty on my own doorstep. And I bet you haven't either.

The grass is always greener, right? Maybe if we just stopped to lie on our own overgrown grass – preferably with a G&T in a plastic cup – we'd realise it's actually pretty lush, and *a whole lot cheaper*.

WHAT *IS* A STAYCATION?

Let's clear this up: I am using the term "staycation" to mean any holiday where you don't need to dust off your passport. That might mean:
- Sleeping in your own bed but clearing your schedule and exploring nearby attractions like a tourist would.

- Booking a couple of nights in a cheap hotel or quirky rental a short drive/train ride away.
- Borrowing a mate's caravan.
- House-sitting for a stranger's cat, tortoise or alpaca. (We have done them all!)
- Packing a tent and a few basic supplies and heading somewhere new.

There are lots of reasons why having a more local holiday could be the right option for you, especially if you have kids. For one, it is less faff. Travelling somewhere local – whether by car, coach or train – is quicker, easier and usually much cheaper than going abroad. If it's your first holiday with a baby or small child, chances are you're already feeling anxious about … well, everything. Being a short drive away from home means less pressure if you forget something "non-essential" that suddenly feels like a lifeline (*Where is the white noise machine?!*). Knowing home is reachable gives you that mental safety net, which is worth its weight in Calpol. Planning a local trip takes far less mental energy than organising a big adventure abroad – and, for many of you, that might be exactly what you need right now.

But beyond the practical perks, one of the biggest reasons to stay local is this: it teaches your kids that holidays aren't about long-haul flights or exotic destinations. They're about *time together*: building blanket forts, exploring somewhere new (even if it's only 20 miles away) and seeing you *actually present*. As parents, we naturally want to do what is "best" for our kids and we often think this means taking them here, there and everywhere. In actual fact, their bar is set pretty low; they just want to have fun with *you*.

Honestly, my sons would take a day of undivided attention, messing about in a muddy stream or camping in the garden over an expensive attraction where I'm glued to my phone. And, if I'm being honest, so would I. After all, the best part about being on holiday is the good vibes and quality time with your loved ones.

AFFORDABLE ACCOMMODATION OPTIONS

You don't need a five-star hotel to have a five-star time. And you don't need to remortgage your house to have a good night away. Whether it's one night in a tent or house-sitting, these experiences are easy on the wallet and big on the memories.

House-sitting

I touched on this earlier in the book, but it makes for a great budget-friendly staycation. You water the plants, feed the pets and, in return, they give you *free accommodation*. Sounds like a scam, but it's not. It usually comes with cute animals, lovely homes and a fun new location. We've done a lot of house-sitting over the years and, honestly, it's one of the best ways to get away without spending much money.

We use a platform that costs around £100 for the year (we share more about our experience on this on our website). That's pretty much your only expense aside from the transport costs to get to each home. Once you're a member, you can apply for "sits". We've stayed in a mansion with a pool, a seaside pad in Brighton and a stunning family home in Devon. One summer, we spent an entire month exploring the south coast of England ... all for that one-off £100 membership fee.

If you land even *one* sit, you've basically paid off the membership. Everything else is a bonus!

Budget stays

There are loads of ways to get that "mini break" feeling without haemorrhaging money.

- **Camping:** Even one night at a local campsite feels like a full-blown adventure when you're with kids. Sleeping in a tent, toasting marshmallows, arguing about guy ropes – it's wholesome chaos, and it costs next to nothing once you have the kit. (The whole of the next chapter is dedicated to camping if this feels like your thing.)
- **Roadside hotels:** Think Travelodge, Premier Inn and Ibis Budget. They're not glamorous, but they are clean, warm and often close

HOW TO HAVE CHEAP FUN AT HOME

Here are easy ways to have fun under your own roof:
- **The blanket fort upgrade:** Not just a fort. Make it a "hotel" – check in at Reception (aka the hallway), hand over a key card (an old loyalty card) and provide room service (biscuits and milk on a tray). Kids love the drama, and you can sneak wine into the "mini-bar".
- **Living room campout:** Ditch the beds for an air mattress or sleeping bags in the lounge. Add fairy lights, popcorn and the rule that *adults* have to ask permission to enter. It feels 100 per cent more exciting than their actual bedroom.
- **Garden camping:** Like real camping, but with flushing toilets and decent Wi-Fi. Let the kids "run wild", then sneak back into your real beds at 2am when the novelty wears off.
- **Local explorer day:** Write a "holiday itinerary" with sightseeing stops in your own town: the park = "botanical gardens", the corner shop = "local market". Bonus points if you throw in ice creams and bad tourist selfies.
- **The "yes day" (with limits):** Let the kids choose the day's activities, but draw the line at buying a pony. Expect a mix of ice cream, the playground and eating cereal for dinner.
- **Around-the-world dinner nights:** Each night is a new "destination" with themed food and music (tacos + "Despacito", pasta + "Mambo Italiano", fish fingers + "Bohemian Rhapsody"). Low effort, high novelty.
- **Travel treasure hunt:** Hide "clues" around the house that lead to the final prize. Works for toddlers *and* teenagers, though teens may roll their eyes at first.

to something vaguely exciting. Book early for the best prices. We've stayed in a Travelodge for £29 a night, and I'm not saying it was luxury, but it did the job – a bed, a clean bathroom and a roof. Find one near a free museum, a beach, a nice park or a splash pad and build a full day of fun around a cheap sleep.
- **Uni dorms (bear with me!):** When students go home for the summer, universities often rent out their rooms. They're usually super cheap and often in city-centre locations. It's not fancy, but it's safe and clean. We did this during the Edinburgh Fringe festival one year and bagged a bargain.
- **Stay with friends or family – but make it an "adventure":** To avoid the "sleeping in Auntie Susan's spare room" energy (no offence to any Auntie Susans out there), treat it like a holiday. Plan day trips, let the kids camp in the living room, bring games and snacks. A change of scene + no cleaning = winning.

STAYCATION ACTIVITIES

What you do during your staycation – and the attitude you bring – will make it or break it. Don't treat it like "just being at home". Lean in. Pretend your town is exotic, your Tesco meal deal is tapas and your local park is basically Central Park (if you squint). Bring the laughs and a *mildly forced sense of enthusiasm* – it'll rub off on the kids eventually.

Explore your patch

- **New town, new vibes:** Visit a nearby town or park you've never set foot in before. You'll be amazed how different somewhere 20 minutes away feels when you decide to call it a "day trip". Bonus points if you get there by bus or coach – suddenly it's an *adventure*, not "just the next town over".
- **DIY treasure hunt:** We once turned a nearby city visit into a quest for "jewels". I'd drop toy gems along the way when Leo wasn't looking, and he thought he'd uncovered ancient treasure. He

buzzed all day, and we got through a walking tour without a single whinge. I felt like an absolute parenting boss.
- **Train + picnic = bliss:** Little kids think trains are rides in themselves. Take a short journey, pack a picnic and the travel becomes the highlight.
- **Hop-on, hop-off fun:** Open-top bus tours are surprisingly brilliant. You see the whole city, the kids will feel like royalty waving at strangers and you don't have to google "things to do" every ten minutes.
- **Theme park hacks:** Theme parks don't have to bankrupt you. Look for two-for-one deals or use supermarket reward points like we do – the smugness of skipping the full ticket price is almost as satisfying as the rides themselves *(see p134 for more theme park tips)*. Alternatively, if money's tight, swap "theme park" for "local swimming pool + McDonald's Happy Meal". Same excitement levels for the kids. Much friendlier for your overdraft.

> **TOP TIP**
> **During the summer, pack a staycation "Go Bag" (for spontaneous days out).**
> Keep a pre-packed crate by the door or in the car so you can bolt when the sun appears. Include: picnic blanket, microfibre towels, swimmers, spare socks, light raincoats, hats, suncream, wet wipes, basic first aid kit, power bank, reusable bottles, a cheap ball and a few emergency snacks. Add coins for parking. Spontaneity is half the fun – this makes it easy!

Have free fun

- **Local libraries:** They often run kids' sessions and crafts. Go and do some activities and then choose some new bedtime stories.
- **Movie night at home:** Pick a film, set up the airbed in the living room, pop some corn and get into those cosy PJs.
- **Geocaching adventures:** It's basically a real-life treasure hunt – and it's totally free and surprisingly addictive. All you need is a

smartphone and the app. Kids *love* it, and it turns even the most "boring" walk into an exciting mission.
- **Nature craft day:** Collect leaves, sticks, flowers and stones, then go full Pinterest: nature crowns, painted rocks, stick people. Low-cost, messy fun and great for little hands.
- **Back garden water park:** When the weather's warm, get out the hose, the paddling pool, some empty washing-up bottles and maybe even a tarp on a slope (go on, live a little). The result? Hours of splashy fun with zero entry fee.
- **Community events and festivals:** Look out for free local fairs, outdoor cinemas, fun days and pop-up markets. Bring a picnic and zero expectations. You might even stumble on a puppet show or a bouncy castle.
- **Free museums and galleries:** Many UK museums, especially in big cities, are completely free and surprisingly kid-friendly. Look out for hands-on zones, interactive trails and even free craft sessions. Pro tip: don't try to see it all. One exhibition and a hot chocolate is plenty. We keep art galleries fun by turning it into a game – like "First to spot a painting with a dog" or "Find the funniest face in a portrait". You could make a "bingo card" and see who can find everything first.
- **Obstacle course challenge:** This is a favourite of ours and you can do it indoors or outside. Use cushions, chairs, string, bean bags and hula hoops. Time each other and award the winner with a small prize (*obviously* make sure everyone wins something to prevent chaos!).

Create traditions

Traditions give your staycations that "This is our thing!" energy – the kind that turns ordinary days into core memories. Here are some lovely (and affordable) ideas you can turn into family classics:
- **Make a "holiday journal" with photos and doodles:** Even if the photos are of you all exploring your local area, you will look back and smile at the time you spent together.

- **Do a back garden campout every summer:** Again, take lots of pictures!
- **Make a "first day of the holiday" breakfast:** Pancakes with sprinkles, chocolate-stuffed croissants or just toast cut into dinosaur shapes – whatever it is, get everyone together for brekkie and make it *the thing* you always do on holiday mornings.
- **Take on the "One new thing" challenge:** Try *one new thing* together on each staycation. It could be as simple as trying a new snack, walking a new trail or learning how to skim a stone. Write it down in your holiday journal or film it.
- **Decorate the house or garden like a mini-resort:** String up bunting, lay out beach towels and pop a cocktail umbrella in your juice. When it becomes tradition, your kids won't care that there's no plane involved – they'll associate it with fun and freedom.
- **Decorate a family holiday flag:** Use old pillowcases, scraps of fabric and marker pens, and raise it on the first day of every staycation, garden campout or local trip. Total nonsense – but pure magic.
- **Make it a tradition to do one generous thing for someone else during your staycation:** Bake something for a neighbour, leave painted rocks on a trail or donate some old toys to a local charity shop. It's a lovely way to teach kids that holidays are about joy *and* kindness.

And don't forget ...
- **Unplug:** Turn off your emails and step away from social media. Put your phone away. Leo absolutely hates seeing me on my phone as he associates it with me working and being unavailable.
- **Treat it like a real holiday (because it is!):** Say yes to double dessert, plan activities and give yourself permission to chill.
- **Splurge on a little something:** That might be breakfast at a café, a round of crazy golf or matching family T-shirts (or maybe not?).

These little rituals might seem silly – pancakes with all the sprinkles, crafting a scrapbook, taking the same daft photo every year – but *this is the stuff* the kids will remember when they look back at their childhood. Not the flight times or hotel star ratings, but the fact that every summer you put up the tent together, or sang that same ridiculous song in the car, or had movie nights in matching pyjamas. And if you've got older kids, it's never too late to start traditions.

Traditions anchor our memories. They tell our kids, *this is what we do; this is who we are.* And when they're grown, they won't remember the mess or the madness – they'll remember how it felt to be part of something fun, familiar and full of love. That's the real magic of a staycation. You're not just saving money – you're building something that lasts way longer than the trip itself.

Want to supercharge that family-bonding magic? Why not swap four walls for fresh air and a tent peg or two. From local fields to European campsites with mobile homes, the next chapter dives into camping: affordable, wild and always unforgettable.

THEME PARK TIPS ON A BUDGET

Theme parks are brilliant for families – they are magical, exciting and full of "wow" moments. They're also a money pit disguised as fun, and, if you don't go in with a plan, you'll leave with sore feet, empty pockets and a child who's livid they didn't get the £18 bubble gun. Here's how to do theme parks *like a pro*, without bankrupting yourself or losing your sanity.

Booking and tickets

- **Book online, *always*:** Even if you're standing at the gate, buy the ticket on your phone. It can still save you £££. At some parks, the "on the day" price is up to 30 per cent more – for the exact same ticket.
- **Check for multi-attraction passes:** Things like Merlin Passes (UK), Paris Explorer Passes or city attraction bundles can save you a fortune if you're visiting more than one attraction over a few days. Some cover SEA LIFE, LEGOLAND® and other big names.
- **Look for Groupon, Wowcher and discount codes:** It's always worth a look, especially in the off-season. Also try websites like Kids Pass or Days Out Guide for free child tickets with train travel.

- **Use your supermarket reward points:** If you shop at certain supermarkets in the UK, the points can build up quickly and can be worth their weight in gold. They can often be exchanged for theme park tickets. Supermarkets around the world have similar loyalty schemes.
- **Check cereal boxes:** The boxes in your food cupboards often have exclusive two-for-one deals or codes that aren't widely advertised.
- **Consider an annual pass:** Annual passes aren't just for diehards. If you live near a park or plan to visit two or three times in a year, a season pass often pays for itself quickly – they often include parking, discounts on food/merch and sneak previews of new rides too.
- **Hotel and ticket bundles:** Weirdly, a package including one night in a budget partner hotel and park entry can occasionally work out *cheaper* than day tickets alone, so it's worth a quick comparison.

Food and drink

- **Bring your own food:** Yes, most parks allow it. Bring sandwiches, fruit, snacks and refillable water bottles – and *treat* the kids to one snack inside like an ice cream or pancakes. It makes the day feel fun without blowing £50 on chicken nuggets and chips.
- **Make use of lockers:** Bring a cool bag with your lunch/snacks and store it in a locker by the entrance. Return at midday for a picnic.

It's like having your own restaurant on standby – without the inflated food bill.
- **Frozen juice boxes double as mini ice packs:** Keeps your lunch cool *and* gives you a cold drink later in the day – peak parenting.
- **Eat early or late:** Take advantage of shorter ride queues while everyone else is hangry and queuing for overpriced pizza.

Think strategically
- **Know the height restrictions *before* you go:** Measure your kids in the morning and steer them away from the rides they can't experience. It's ultimately better they never see it as an option than sob in front of it. Most theme parks will have an app where you can filter rides by height requirement, too.
- **Choose your park wisely:** Some theme parks are brilliant for toddlers (like Gulliver's in the UK), while others are aimed at much older kids (like Thorpe Park in the UK). A "meh" park for your child's age = wasted money and tears.
- **Consider accessibility:** Many parks offer passes for neurodiverse children or those with additional needs. Ask at guest services for support and to find out what's on offer.
- **Get the app:** Most parks have one and they offer real-time wait times, park maps and mobile ordering for food. It's a lifesaver – especially when you've walked in a circle three times trying to find the loo.

- **Parent swap:** Many rides will offer what's called a parent swap (sometimes called baby swap). Basically, it means the parents can have fun too, even if the kids are too small for the big rollercoasters. You only need to queue once and then swap your kids over with the other parent/adult as you exit the ride.
- **Pack a towel and change of clothes:** Even if you're not doing water rides, someone *will* get wet. Leo recently stood in the "splash zone" of a huge log flume – he was drenched and we hadn't brought a change of clothes for him. Learn from our mistakes!
- **Bring mini fans and ponchos:** Theme parks are extreme environments – it will either be boiling hot or raining sideways on the day you visit, guaranteed. Dress accordingly. Pound-shop ponchos will save you £15 on the branded ones being sold in the park.
- **Get your kids to wear wristbands with your number:** If your kids are runners or easily distracted, stick a paper wristband on them with your phone number.
- **Use lockers strategically:** Many parks have lockers that you can access all day with a code. Share one, dump everything bulky and *don't* try to carry everything around "just in case". You'll regret it by lunchtime.
- **Evening parade = ride time:** If you don't care about the parade/fireworks, that's prime time for the shortest ride queues. If you *do* care,

watch from near the exit – that way, you'll beat the post-parade stampede to get out.

Niche but genius tips
- **Go left:** Don't ask me why, but most people turn right when they enter a park. *You* go left. The left-side rides are usually quieter first thing.
- **Plan your route backwards:** Go to the biggest, furthest ride early – while everyone else is queuing at the flashy one near the entrance.
- **Let kids nap in the queue:** If you have a buggy-age child, use their nap time as the perfect time to join that long queue. This is perfect if there are two adults: one of you queues while the other sits in peace with the sleeping child. Then use parent swap once at the front. It buys you a bit of peace and flexibility later.
- **Pack glow sticks:** Buy them for £1 beforehand and whip them out when it gets dark. You'll look like a budget hero when all the £20 light-up toys come out and your kid already has a self-made glowing sword.

- **Buy second-hand merch before you go:** The stuff kids beg for inside the park – bubble wands, Minnie ears, lightsabres – is *everywhere* on Vinted, eBay or Facebook Marketplace for a fraction of the price. Pack them secretly, then "magically" hand them over midway through the day. Kids think you caved; you save £40.
- **Bring a bubble gun *and* extra bubble liquid:** They are *so* much cheaper when you buy them in advance and will give them hours of fun. They also make for great entertainment if you want to queue for a "big" ride that they can't go on.
- **Make use of rainy-day guarantees:** Some parks offer free return visits if it rains heavily. Check the small print – and keep your receipts. Even if you have a great day in the rain, you may as well come back if it's free!

Chapter Seven
CLEVER CAMPING

Hopefully by now I've convinced you that you don't need a five-star resort and bottomless piña coladas to have a *real* holiday. It can be as simple as sourcing a tent, a camping hob and kettle (essential) and the ability to laugh-cry when it inevitably chucks it down. Camping and holiday parks are seriously underrated – and not just because of the price.

Our first ever time camping as parents was … bold. Leo was just 12 weeks old, and we weren't heading to a sleepy little campsite with sheep and silence – we were off to Glastonbury Festival, one of the biggest music festivals on the planet. We'd secured those golden tickets before we really grasped just how *extra* tent life with a newborn could be. But we were excited, naive and raring to give it a go. They had family camping fields, a baby tent with baby bath time and lots of healthcare staff on site – it sounded ideal.

Here's the thing: a lack of experience and a healthy dose of naivety can work in your favour when it comes to family travel. We showed up blissfully unaware that we'd need to work fairly hard to keep our baby alive in a $2m^2$ sauna. Because it was *hot*. And I don't mean "Ooh, better crack open a window" hot. I mean 30°C (86°F)-plus, inside a tent, armed only with a handheld fan and a few wet towels. Let's just say the room temperature was not within the NHS-approved 16–20°C (61–68°F) ideal for babies. Not even close. We had one of those glowing egg thermometers that constantly reminded us that it was, indeed, too hot. Luckily, we came armed with lots of little muslin cloths, which we soaked and laid over Leo like he was a tiny Michelin-starred burrata. We shaded the pram, rigged up extra cover wherever we sat and managed to survive. Actually, scrap that – we thrived and had an amazing time. (Exhausting and sweaty, but genuinely amazing.)

Moral of the story? When camping with little ones, go prepared for *all* weather. Especially in the UK, where there can be monsoon-level downpours and scorching sunshine on the same day. And remember, in the worst-case scenario, you can just drive home.

WHY CHOOSE CAMPING OR HOLIDAY PARKS?

Camping is the OG budget holiday. We're not talking *Lord of the Flies* with toddlers. We're talking toast under the stars, swimming pools, kids' discos plus no one judging your messy hair and Crocs. Camping in a tent is very different to camping in a mobile home. There's a range of options available, and you can lower yourself in gradually if needed. Here are some of the benefits of outdoor life:

- **Affordability:** Campsites and holiday parks often cost a fraction of what you'd pay for a hotel. Even glamping can come out cheaper if you shop around or travel off-peak.
- **Closer to nature:** Wake up to birdsong, fall asleep to a gentle breeze ... and yes, probably a few suspicious rustles in the bushes too. It's all part of the charm.
- **Screentime reset:** Wi-Fi is usually patchy at best. Annoying for Instagram, brilliant for prising kids off iPads and convincing them to play swing-ball instead.
- **Facilities and entertainment:** Lots of holiday parks have pools, kids' clubs, splash zones and more entertainment than you'll know what to do with.
- **Built-in community:** Campsites are crawling with families. Kids make instant friends, and parents get that magical 20 minutes of peace while someone else's child teaches yours how to climb a tree.
- **Kids love it:** Mud. Freedom. Other feral children to run wild with.

CAMPING KIT: BUY, BORROW OR BAG A BARGAIN

Camping kit can get *expensive*, fast. But it doesn't have to. Here are some ways to keep the costs down:

THE TRIAL RUN: GARDEN CAMPING

Before you go full Bear Grylls, borrow a tent, dig out those torches and pitch up in your own back garden. It's the safest way to discover:

- If your kids are into it
- If your back is into it (consider an air mattress over a roll mat)
- If your tent is actually waterproof (a garden hose test counts as science)
- Whether you remembered to pack anything useful
- How fun bedtime is when you forget to bring the teddies/nightlights/entire routine

It's better to find out all this at home than at midnight in the Lake District while the baby cries and your partner googles "symptoms of a nervous breakdown".

- **Borrow first:** Ask your mates, your neighbour, your cousin's ex – odds are someone has a tent gathering dust in the garage.
- **Scour second-hand marketplaces:** Gumtree, Facebook Marketplace, Vinted, car boot sales – they are all crawling with nearly new camping gear from people who used it *once* and then remembered they prefer all-inclusive.
- **Rifle through charity shops in affluent areas:** Honestly, you'd be shocked by what turns up. Fold-up camping tables, sleeping bags and even fancy blow-up mattresses – all at gloriously low prices.

- **Check out Decathlon and Aldi's Special Buys aisle:** These are two absolute havens for budget camping gear. Decathlon especially has starter kits for families that won't bankrupt you.
- **Don't forget "Freecycle" or "Buy Nothing" groups:** People often give away bulky items just to get them out of the shed. You could kit out a whole trip for the price of a "thank you" message.
- **Rent it:** If you're only camping once a year, renting can save you money (and cupboard space). Many campsites offer tents, cooking gear or even full setups ready and waiting for you when you arrive – no faff, no packing. Just double-check the size when you book. We once hired a "two-man tent" for my parents that was so small, a baby on a lilo would've struggled to fit inside.
- **Split the cost with friends:** If you've got fellow camping-curious mates or family, go in together on big items like a decent tent or cooking stove and rotate who uses it.

And remember, it's not just the big stuff that adds up. Don't forget about:

- **Power banks:** Essential if you want your maps app or *Cocomelon*.
- **Lanterns or head torches:** Don't forget *actual* working batteries too, not the ones that died in your TV remote and never made it to the bin.
- **Spare tent pegs:** Trust me, you'll lose half by day two.
- **A corkscrew:** Because wine may be needed.

You don't need to splash out on every gadget in the Go Outdoors showroom. Keep it simple, ask around and start small. Once you have the kit, you will have tons of opportunities for a cheap getaway.

FINDING THE PERFECT SPOT

Deciding where to camp is really important. Pitch in the wrong place and your 'peaceful escape to nature' can turn into a 3am rave courtesy of next door's inflatable hot tub.

Choosing the right campsite

Not all campsites are created equal. Some feel like family holiday heaven; others are basically a field with a bin. When camping with kids, look for:
- **Toilets you'd actually use:** Proper toilet blocks over compost loos hidden in a hedge. Midnight toilet trips are bad enough without needing a head torch and a strong stomach.
- **Hot showers:** Not "warm if you feed it a £1 coin every 30 seconds". Actual hot showers. For everyone's sake.
- **Built-in entertainment:** Playgrounds, pools, maybe even a kids' disco. The more options for tiring them out, the better your chance of finishing a book (or at least a drink).
- **Family-friendly pricing:** Kids-go-free deals or family discounts. Camping should be cheap; if the nightly price makes you gasp, move along.
- **Location:** Don't go too remote. A nearby town (or at least a Lidl) saves you from paying £6 for a bag of marshmallows at the campsite shop.

Choosing the right pitch

A pitch is not *just* a patch of grass. It's your kingdom for the weekend – your basecamp, your kitchen, your bedroom and (if the rain kicks in) your family-sized panic room. So, choosing the *right* one can make or break your camping experience. Here's what to consider (and what to avoid at all costs):
- **Right next to the loos = no thanks:** It *sounds* convenient – until you realise the loos are busy all night, the hand dryer is louder than a jet engine and every toddler in the campsite is on a synchronised 2am toilet schedule. Not to mention the fragrant breeze. You've been warned.
- **Miles from the loos = also no:** Especially if you've got small kids or a weak bladder (or both?). A midnight dash through wet grass while carrying a half-asleep four-year-old who "can't hold it", while trying not to trip over a maze of guy ropes, is an Olympic sport no one asked to compete in.

- **Avoid the wind tunnel:** You might laugh now, but nothing wipes the smug off your face like watching your tent flap itself inside-out at 2am. Check the direction of prevailing winds if you're coastal or exposed, and look for natural shelter like hedges, bushes or trees (as long as they're sturdy and not shedding branches).
- **Pick flat ground – always:** It sounds obvious, but when you're tired and everyone's hangry you might overlook that subtle slope ... until you wake up with the whole family squashed into a corner and your toddler using your face as a pillow.
- **Shade is your friend:** Especially in the summer. Tents heat up like ovens and there is *nothing* worse than being woken at 6am, sweating in your sleeping bag like a soggy sausage roll. Trees or partial shade = lifesaver.
- **Check the surface:** Grass is ideal. Gravel? Less so. Rocky ground? Nightmare. Mud pit? Hard pass.
- **Look around you:** Avoid pitching at the bottom of a hill – unless you fancy waking up in a puddle after a bit of rain. And steer clear of major footpaths or cut-throughs if you don't want every kid on a scooter zooming past your guy ropes.

MY ULTIMATE CAMPING PACKING TIPS

Packing for a family camping trip is an adventure in itself. You're not just throwing a few clothes in a bag – you're basically building a tiny, semi-functional version of your home ... in bags ... for the outdoors ... with children. It's no joke. You're not just packing for a weekend away; you're packing for every possible disaster nature – and your children – can throw at you. You have to assume there are no shops, there's no electricity and someone *will* spill juice, lose a shoe or shit their pants – at least once during the trip (and that's not even counting what the kids might do). It sounds chaotic (and it *is*), but with the right prep, you can avoid major disasters and maybe even enjoy yourself. Here's a well-rounded, trauma-tested list of what to pack to give yourself the best chance at survival – and maybe even a good time.

Layers, layers, layers

Even if the weather app promises consistent sunshine, don't believe it.
- **Pack a jumper, thermal tops and cosy PJs:** Yes, even in August. One minute you're roasting marshmallows in a vest top, the next you're lying awake at 3am, teeth chattering, seriously considering whether hypothermia is covered by your travel insurance.
- **Don't forget socks:** Lots of socks. Some will be wet, some will go missing, some will be worn as gloves in desperation.
- **A waterproof coat for everyone is essential:** Once you're wet, you're *wet*. Trying to dry clothes in the rain is like trying to grill a sausage with a hairdryer.

Torches and headlamps

Every child needs their own torch or headlamp. Not because they'll use them responsibly, but because they'll *definitely* fight over them otherwise. Who needs expensive gadgets when you can shine a torch on the tent wall? Bring lots of spare batteries too, because someone will undoubtedly leave the torch on all night.

> **TOP TIP**
> **Pack lots of bin bags.**
> Not glamorous, but glorious. Honestly, bin bags might be the unsung heroes of your packing list. Use them for wet clothes, rubbish, dirty shoes, emergency picnic blankets and even makeshift ponchos. You'll think you brought too many. You didn't.

First aid kit

This is a must. Kids fall, parents stub toes on tent pegs and someone always ends up with nettle rash or a suspicious bite. Pack it like you're the camp medic (because you are):
- **Savlon, Sudocrem or a multipurpose antiseptic cream:** For bites, stings, scrapes and pretty much anything you don't like the look of.
- **Suncream:** Easy to forget, expensive to replace. We've made the mistake of leaving it behind on UK trips and ended up paying triple at the campsite shop.

- **Hand sanitiser / antiseptic wipes:** For cleaning grubby hands before you can even *get* to the plasters. Essential in muddy fields.
- **Plasters – loads of them, and make them waterproof:** Not just those tiny ones either – assorted sizes. And bring *more than you think you'll need*. Brownie points if they've got cartoons, dinosaurs, fairies or animals on them.
- **Microporous tape and gauze:** For when someone manages to bleed in a way no plaster was designed for.
- **Mosquito spray:** Because prevention is better than cure.
- **Antihistamines – liquid and tablets:** Because someone will touch a plant they shouldn't or get bitten by a mutant insect. Bonus points if you also pack hydrocortisone cream for the inevitable itchy aftermath.
- **Calpol / Nurofen for kids:** Bring the sachets *and* the bottle. And the syringe. And a backup syringe, because the original will vanish into a bag pocket somewhere just as someone spikes a fever.
- **Tweezers:** Not for vanity – for splinters, thorns, stingers and that weird bit of gravel embedded in someone's knee.
- **Tick remover tool:** If you're camping anywhere remotely wild, ticks are not a hypothetical problem. They are very real, and very gross. I once pulled 16 from behind my knee … Russian roulette but with Lyme disease.
- **Rehydration sachets:** Mainly for if (when?) you have one too many plastic-cup wines and forget to hydrate properly.
- **Blister plasters:** Because someone (usually me) *will* wear new trainers for a hike that they swear are comfy, and then hobble dramatically for the next 48 hours.
- **Sterile saline pods:** Good for flushing out eyes full of dirt, bug spray or toddler-applied sun cream.
- **Thermometer:** Don't try to guess your kid's temperature. You'll either panic over a sweaty forehead or ignore a very high fever thinking it's "just the weather".

- **Burn gel or dressings:** For when your child decides to wave a flaming marshmallow on a stick directly past their sibling's face, almost branding them with molten sugar.

And don't forget:
- If your child has allergies, bring their meds, EpiPens, if prescribed, and a printed prescription or care plan in case of emergencies. If you are staying far from medical help, multiple EpiPens can quite literally be a lifesaver.
- Know where the nearest hospital or urgent care centre is. Save it on your phone. *Then screenshot it.* Because signal always disappears when you most need it.
- Pack the kit in a waterproof bag, and *keep it somewhere accessible.* Not buried under seven towels and a box of cereal.

Sleeping comfort

Forget that romantic idea of "roughing it" on the ground – you're a parent now.

- **Decent roll mats, self-inflating mats or, better yet, airbeds:** Believe me, these are worth investing in. And don't forget a pump! João once blew a double airbed up with his mouth. I would have been sleeping on the floor if it was down to me.
- **Sleeping bags:** If you want that cosy "home from home" vibe, you could even pack a quilt.
- **Pillows:** I mean actual pillows, not camping pillows – getting a decent sleep is essential for you enjoying this trip.
- **Extra blankets:** For when it gets cold overnight – you can even buy sleeping bag liners.

Kitchen kit

This is where it's easy to overpack or forget something vital – like the kettle. (*Don't* forget the kettle.) There are so many camping gadgets that it can be overwhelming knowing what to take. With the below items, you will be well away.

- **A basic camping stove or portable hob:** Always bring a spare gas canister.
- **Pans to cook with:** Camping ones that slot inside each other are great for space saving.
- **A kettle or small pan:** For boiling water (for coffee, washing up and the all-important Pot Noodle).
- **A collapsible washing-up bowl:** Don't forget a sponge and biodegradable washing-up liquid.
- **Cutlery, plates, bowls and mugs:** Preferably non-breakable. We like to take more than we need so we're not reliant on washing up after every single meal.
- **Cooking essentials:** Think a chopping board, a sharp knife, a wooden spoon, a bottle opener and a tin opener – you'll always forget the tin opener.
- **Condiment stash:** Tiny sachets of ketchup, mayo, salt and pepper.
- **A collapsible water container:** Most sites have a tap, but it's rarely next to your tent.
- **Tea towels:** Bring more than one. One will be used for the dishes; one will act as a makeshift oven mitt; one will get used to clean up the spilled wine; and one will mysteriously vanish into the void.
- **A cooler box or thermal bag:** To keep milk, butter or snacks from melting or curdling.
- **Camping chairs and table:** These may sound extra, but your ageing back will thank you.

Food and snacks

Don't rely on campsite cafés – they're either closed, cash-only or sell a ham sandwich for £6.

- **Pack simple, low-effort food:** Think cereal bars, instant noodles, pasta, porridge sachets, UHT milk, apples and Babybels.
- **Bring more snacks than you think is humanly necessary:** We all know a well-timed snack can prevent a full-blown meltdown (for both adults and kids).

- **Marshmallows and chocolate digestives for s'mores:** Finding a wild stick to roast your marshmallow is a thing of childhood wonder – followed by adult regret when it immediately catches fire and flings molten sugar onto someone's Crocs. Then no one wants to eat it because it smells bad.

Baby and toddler essentials

If you're travelling with littler ones, add these:
- **Potty training gear (if applicable):** Travel potty, plenty of biodegradable wet wipes, nappies and nappy sacks. Don't forget the nappy sacks.
- **Travel high chair:** You can buy foldable travel high chairs or use a booster seat you can strap to a camping chair.
- **Travel cot or sleep pod:** Something familiar helps with night-time routines.
- **Your child's favourite toys:** Pack as many as possible.
- **A nightlight or portable white noise machine:** Or your phone if you're brave with battery life.

> **TOP TIP**
> **Secure the baby!**
> Consider taking a play pen or wind breakers to make a secure area for mobile babies.

Clothing and footwear

- **At least two outfits per day per child:** Be prepared for mud, water, ketchup – the classics.
- **Waterproof footwear:** Wellies or waterproof shoes for outdoors; Crocs or sliders for showers.
- **Swimsuits and towels:** Even if there's no pool, water play always happens somewhere.
- **A spare change of clothes for everyone:** Keep a dry change of clothes in the car for you all, just in case – you will thank me one day.

Miscellaneous must-haves

- **Clothes line and pegs:** Perfect for drying wet clothes and towels – and helps to avoid that slightly damp smell in your tent.
- **Dry shampoo, a flannel and/or biodegradable wet wipes = your hygiene plan:** If you *think* you'll shower daily, that's cute. You won't. Bring wet wipes and a flannel, and lower your standards. Bring two flannels if you want a face one and a "miscellaneous body" one. Label accordingly or live dangerously.
- **Hand sanitiser and loo roll:** Some campsites provide it, many mysteriously do not.
- **Earplugs:** Pack these for everyone. Tents are loud. People snore. Birds wake up at 4am. Someone nearby *might* play "Wonderwall" on a guitar or, even worse, a ukulele. Earplugs are the thin line between sleep and tears.
- **A mallet:** Using your shoe to whack in a reluctant tent peg is never a great idea.
- **A roll of duct tape:** It fixes tents. It fixes chairs. It fixes shoes. One day you'll need it and feel like Bear Grylls when you pull it out from the bottom of your bag.
- **Games:** Card games or mini board games for when it inevitably rains; bats and balls for outdoor activities.

It might sound like a lot, but the key is organisation. Use packing cubes, clear boxes or IKEA bags to group similar items – food in one, bedding in another, chaos in a third. That way, you can grab what you need without rooting through a black hole of socks and random plastic dinosaurs.

HOLIDAY PARKS: CAMPING BUT MORE POSH

If everything I've said so far fills you with dread, then holiday parks might just be your budget-friendly saviour. You still get the fun of being outdoors, the family-friendly vibe and the freedom to let your kids run semi-feral, but without the part where you sleep in a tent.

Holiday parks are basically camping's boujee upgrade. No soggy socks. No tent faff. You get a genuine roof, a proper bed and maybe even a hot tub if you're lucky.

What to expect

Holiday parks have come a long way since soggy tents and communal showers. These days, they're more "budget-friendly resort" than "Boy Scouts with blisters". Whether you're after a cosy glamping pod or a lodge with all the mod cons, there's something for every kind of family (and every kind of parent, from nature-loving to *needs-Wi-Fi-at-all-times*). Picture comfort for you, chaos for them, and enough distractions that you might actually finish a brew while it's still hot. Here's what's typically on offer:

- **Accommodation options galore:** Think static caravans, glamping pods or safari tents – all the fun of the outdoors, but with plug sockets and mattresses that don't make you want to cry.
- **Facilities on site:** Forget "walking to the tap with a washing-up bowl" – you will have your own kitchen with lots to do on site. Holiday parks often have:
  - Splash pools and indoor water parks
  - Mini golf, climbing walls, trampolines
  - Arcades where your child will spend £10 trying to win a 30p bouncy ball
  - Spas (for the 30 seconds you may or may not get to yourself)
  - Restaurants, bars and cafés
- **Organised activities:** From toddler yoga to family karaoke, most parks run a full timetable of "stuff to do" so you don't have to plan anything too taxing:
  - Craft sessions, mini discos, outdoor cinema nights
  - Bingo that gets weirdly competitive (don't underestimate the nan with her own glittery dobber)
  - Waterslides your kids will go down 73 times until they are burned to a crisp and have to be pulled away kicking and screaming

Finding the best prices

There are loads of ways to keep things thrifty – if you know where to look. With a bit of planning, you can save serious money and still have a trip that feels anything but budget. Here's how to bag the best deals without sacrificing the fun (or your sanity):

- **Avoid peak school holiday dates like your life depends on it:** Easier said than done I realise. But the difference in price between the last week of August and the first week of September is basically a mortgage payment. If your kids can miss a few days of school, either side of any of the school holidays, you will save *a lot* of money.
- **Sign up to newsletters:** Places like Eurocamp, Haven, Parkdean and, naturally, The Travel Mum often do early-bird discounts, flash sales or cheeky discount codes that'll knock a nice chunk off your total.
- **Travel in shoulder seasons (May, June and September) for:**
  - Lower prices
  - Smaller crowds
  - Better availability
  - Slightly smug feelings when you post photos and no one else is on the beach
- **If you're booking Eurocamp-style, check prices between countries:** It might be cheaper to visit a destination that hasn't been on your radar.
- **Play with your dates:** Even shifting your holiday by one or two days can make a huge difference in price. Midweek departures are often cheaper than weekends.
- **Join relevant Facebook groups or forums:** There are entire communities dedicated to finding travel bargains. People share promo codes, flash deals or insider tips you won't see elsewhere – and you can ask real people about their experiences too.
- **Be flexible on location within the park:** Premium pitches and "sea view" upgrades sound nice, but can be a massive upsell. Opting for a basic cabin or being a three-minute walk from the pool

could save you a fortune – and still give you the same access to everything on site.
- **Book early or super late:** Early birds usually get the best prices and the widest choice. But, if you're brave (and flexible), last-minute deals can also be absolute steals. This works best if you're happy to go wherever the best price is.

> **TOP TIP**
> **Check for air con (seriously, check).**
> In southern Europe air con is not guaranteed, but it is very much needed! If you've never tried to put an overtired, sweaty toddler to bed in a 40°C (104°F) caravan that feels like a Tupperware container placed in hell ... well, don't. Always check the fine print or filter for "air conditioning" before you book. If there's no air con, ask if fans are provided. It may be cheaper to book without AC, but in the summer, just don't do it.

Budgeting for holiday parks

Between the arcades, overpriced snacks and the on-site shop that charges £4 for a single loo roll, it's easy to blow the budget without realising. The good news? With a few clever tricks and a bit of planning, you can keep things firmly in the "bargain break" zone without missing out on the fun. Here's how to make your money go further (so you can save it for what really matters – like extra wine or a rainy-day emergency slush fund):

- **Self-cater to save a fortune:** Pack your own snacks, breakfast bits and a few easy dinner options *(see the self-catering recipe ideas on p74)*. Even just avoiding the café toasties and ice creams every day will save you a small fortune. Bonus points for bringing a slow cooker or air fryer if you're driving and there's room in the car.
- **Limit arcade visits – set a "fun budget":** Give the kids a set amount each day (in coins or tokens) and, when it's gone, it's gone. Explain that having "only" £5 to win a 30p bouncy ball builds character. Or bring your own prizes and let them "cash out" at your own mum-run prize counter with better exchange rates.

- **Free stuff is your best friend:** Holiday parks often include pools, kids' clubs, outdoor play areas, nature trails and beach access at no extra charge. Plan your day around these and use the paid extras as occasional treats, not daily routines.
- **Bring the basics from home:** I'm talking washing-up liquid, bin bags, loo roll, tea towels, kitchen roll, washing-up sponges, hand soap – the lot. Buy it in your weekly shop and avoid paying resort prices for absolute essentials.
- **Pack entertainment:** Bring board games, colouring books, footballs and even a few rainy-day surprises from the pound shop. That way, you're not scrambling to buy overpriced toys or activities every time the weather turns.
- **Share costs with friends or family:** Booking a larger lodge or caravan and splitting the cost with another family can work out *way* cheaper per person – plus, the kids entertain each other and you might actually get to finish a sentence (or a drink).
- **Check what's actually included:** Some activities and evening entertainment may come at an extra cost. Double-check in advance so you're not caught off guard, and see if there's a wristband or activity pass that covers multiple things for less.
- **BYOB (bring your own booze):** Bars on site can be expensive. Bring your own drinks and enjoy a cheeky G&T on your porch instead. A big bottle of squash for the kids also goes a long way (and keeps them away from £4-a-pop slushies).
- **Meal plan – loosely:** You don't need a military-style spreadsheet, but having a rough idea of what you'll eat each day helps avoid the "We've got nothing in, let's just eat out again" trap. Even having cereal and pasta in the cupboard keeps things flexible and cheap.
- **Use loyalty points and vouchers:** Tesco Clubcard, Nectar points, Blue Light Card, Kids Pass – they can all go surprisingly far when it comes to booking or buying extras. Check if your park partners with any reward schemes.

- **Book extras in advance:** If you *do* want to try a paid activity like pony trekking, crazy golf or a spa treatment, you can often book ahead for less. It also helps you stick to your budget without getting caught up in "but pleeeease" persuasion tactics once you arrive.

Camping and holiday parks offer freedom, affordability and fun – your kids are more likely to remember the chaos of a camping trip over a perfectly curated luxury hotel stay. You *can* make these holidays amazing without breaking the bank or your spirit. Just plan smart, pack the basics and lower your standards for cleanliness just a *tad*.

Of course, not every family adventure starts with a suitcase full of toys. For some, the journey begins much earlier – when you're travelling with a bump. Part Three is all about navigating the different stages of family travel, starting with pregnancy.

EASY CAMPING WITH KIDS

1. **Use packing cubes:** One per person. These make finding what everyone needs super easy. Have one for dirty clothes too.
2. **Don't forget the glow products:** Glow sticks on kids after dark = genius. They'll love it and you'll always spot them.
3. **Blackout tents for the win:** No one wants to be woken up by the summer sun at 5am.
4. **Bring a bucket with a lid:** 3am wees made easy.
5. **Don't over-schedule:** Let the magic come from mucking about outdoors.

GLOBAL CAMPING IDEAS

Camping is a worldwide wonder, whether you're pitching a tent in the forest or glamping under the stars with a glass of wine in one hand and a baby bottle in the other. Here are some family-friendly places to roll out your sleeping bags:

Canada
Think mountains, lakes, wildlife – and probably the nicest campsite neighbours you'll ever meet.
- **Banff** and **Jasper National Parks** are very family-friendly with ranger programmes and easy trails.
- Provincial parks across **Ontario** and **British Columbia** also offer amazing (and less crowded) alternatives.

Croatia
If you want seaside views without the price tag of Italy or Greece, Croatia is your place.
- **Istria** and **Dalmatia** are dotted with coastal campsites – some even have water parks on site.
- Look for **Valamar campsites** – they're known for family-friendly facilities and beautiful locations.

France
France is the OG of family camping holidays. Sites here are basically mini-resorts with pools, waterslides, kids' clubs and actual baguettes delivered to your pitch.

- **Eurocamp:** These are all over the country, from the Loire Valley to the Med coast, and are perfect for first-timers. We like the La Croix du Vieux Pont camp and its ideal location for Disneyland and Paris.
- **Huttopia:** Stylish and nature-focused, these campsites have a chilled-out vibe and fab locations near rivers, forests and lakes.
- **Les Castels:** Often set in castle grounds (yes, really), these sites are a mix of luxury and nature. Think: croissants in your PJs and a château behind you.

Italy

Italy is your perfect base for great campsites, beautiful scenery and child-loving locals – in fact, it's a pizza-fuelled paradise. Many Italian campsites also offer animation teams (think kids' discos, games and more), so you can actually finish your Aperol spritz in peace.

- **Lake Garda** and **Tuscany** are top picks. We stayed at a park near Lake Garda and loved exploring lakeside towns and visiting Gardaland Resort theme park.
- Try **Camping Village Fabulous** just outside Rome for a blend of poolside fun and Roman ruins.

Japan

Japan is surprisingly underrated for camping, but is great if you want to mix nature with culture. You usually need to book ahead.

- Family-friendly sites in the **Japanese Alps** or by **Mount Fuji** are scenic and well-equipped.
- Many sites offer quirky extras like BBQ huts, hot springs and actual toilets.

Netherlands
The Netherlands is super safe, flat (so great for cycling) and offers surprisingly cool campsites.
- **De Krim Texel** is fantastic for families – with beaches, wildlife and all the Dutch vibes.
- **Duinrell** has a theme park *and* a water park on site.

New Zealand
This is a dream destination for road trips and camping.
- Loads of **DOC (Department of Conservation) sites** are cheap, simple and set in gorgeous surroundings.
- Camper vans are super popular and great for families.

Portugal
This has it all: warm weather, golden beaches and family-friendly sites.
- **The Algarve** has some great camping options – from rustic, rural vibes to bigger parks with pools and entertainment.
- **Costa Vicentina** is wilder, more rugged and less touristy – perfect for nature lovers.
- Try **Orbitur** or **Yelloh! Village** sites for easy, family-approved stays.

Spain
Sun, sand and sangria ...
- Look out for sites near **Barcelona** or **Valencia** for a city-meets-beach combo.
- The **Costa Brava** and **Costa Dorada** are packed with seaside campsites that come with pools, beach access and excellent food.

- Many offer mobile homes or pre-pitched tents for maximum ease with minimum faff.

Sweden and Norway

Wild camping is legal in both, but don't go in blind.
- **Sweden** has lots of areas where you can wild camp for free, and many towns offer basic but clean pitches near lakes and forests.
- **Norway** is a dream for road trips in summer – you can pitch your tent in stunning spots by fjords, waterfalls or mountains. Just follow the rules and leave no trace.

USA

As with everything in America, this is camping done *big*. We haven't actually camped in the USA, but it is high on our wish list!
- National parks like **Yosemite**, **Yellowstone** and **Zion** are bucket list-worthy, but you'll need to book months in advance.
- Many sites are basic but set in jaw-dropping scenery, perfect for older kids who can handle the adventure.

TOP TIP
If you're hitting more than one US national park, look into the America the Beautiful Pass.
It covers entry to over 2,000 federal sites (including the big-name parks) and usually pays for itself after two or three visits.

MY TOP 10 SUSTAINABLE TRAVEL TIPS

Over-tourism is a growing issue in many destinations, but that doesn't mean you have to shelve your travel dreams or drown in guilt every time you book a flight. None of us are perfect, but, if we all travel with a bit more awareness and intention, it can make a big difference. Little swaps = big ripples.

Bring your children into the decision-making too – let them help pick greener routes, buy second-hand gear and support local businesses. Explain why only taking what you need is important and why public transport is better than a taxi – you're not just planning a trip; you're raising mindful travellers!

1. **Choose off-the-beaten-path destinations:** Swap tourist-saturated hotspots for hidden gems. You'll dodge the crowds *and* your money will mean more to the local economy.
2. **Spend money with local businesses:** Eat at family-run restaurants, stay in locally owned guesthouses and book experiences with real people, not faceless corporations. Spending with local businesses ensures your money stays within the communities you are visiting and benefits the local people. We recently visited some local islands within the Maldives. Spending our money at small local restaurants meant experiencing life as a local and getting to eat yummy authentic food at a fraction of resort prices.
3. **Support destinations that really benefit from tourism:** Some regions rely heavily on visitors to keep local businesses alive. Rural areas, lesser-known towns and places recovering from tough times (like natural disasters) often get overlooked in favour of big-name resorts. Choosing them for your family trip not only benefits your budget but also makes a real difference to the people who live there.

4. **Travel in the shoulder or off-season:** You'll avoid the peak-season stampede, lower your impact and usually score better prices.
5. **Use public transport where you can:** Trains, buses, coaches, ferries and bicycles are way more sustainable than hiring a car or taking a dozen short flights. Bonus: you'll get a better taste of local life too.
6. **Choose eco-conscious accommodation:** Green creds aren't just a potted plant in Reception. Look for the real stuff: solar panels, refillable toiletries, recycling bins, water-saving showers – these all show that a place is really trying.
7. **Pack light and avoid plastic:** Overpacking = more weight = more fuel. Plus, take a reusable water bottle and tote bag to avoid single-use plastics.
8. **Respect the locals and their culture:** Sustainability isn't just about the environment – it's about people too. Be kind, ask questions, learn a few words in the local language and don't be *that* tourist.
9. **Book low-emission flights:** When you need to fly, try to make the lower-carbon choice. Pick non-stop routes (take-off/landing burn the most fuel), fly economy and pack light. Use emissions filters on flight search tools and skip short hops you could do by train or coach.
10. **Bundle trips:** Fly less often, stay longer. Consider having a longer trip rather than multiple small ones. Offsetting can be a plus, but it isn't a free pass.

Part Three
GROWING TOGETHER

This part of the book has been the hardest for me to write – not because I don't remember it, but because I remember it *so clearly*. The trauma is real. The joy. The grief. The hope. The fear. The absolute emotional rollercoaster that came with something that, for most people, seems so simple. IVF treatment, infertility and pregnancy loss is no joke. Unless you have been through it, you can't fully appreciate the trauma. And if you're in the thick of it now, please consider this a gentle warning. What follows might be too close, too raw – please think of yourself and skip past this introduction and get straight into the chapters themselves.

The thing is, we're expected to carry on through it all. To smile politely at dinner parties. To show up to work like we didn't cry in the car on the way there. To post cute pictures online while quietly falling apart behind the screen. We grieve in silence, often cloaked in shame – as if our bodies failing us is something we should hide. And yet it's so common. Too common.

As you'll know from Part One, Leo was a very welcome surprise. A new relationship, no effort and boom – I was a mum. We always knew we wanted to give him a sibling, but, as you read in Part Two, life got in the way. When we did finally start "properly" trying, I never expected it would be difficult. I definitely didn't expect it to *test me* like it did.

What started as hopeful anticipation became months of disappointment. Then years. Uncertainty crept in, then fear, then heartbreak. We were fighting a battle for something we had zero control over. Eventually, we began IVF – a last-resort lifeline that completely took over our lives, emotionally and financially. Everything else was put on hold. We were stuck in a loop – hope, heartbreak, repeat. Every negative test chipped away at me. I'd break them open, squinting at the strip of paper, desperate for a flicker of blue. "Maybe it's too early," I'd whisper. Then my period would come. Hope gone. Heart broken. Repeat.

The Travel Mum became my escape, my lifeline. I didn't know anyone in real life who'd gone through IVF, but I found women online who *got it*. They were total strangers, and yet they understood better than anyone else. They knew the waiting, the hoping and the crushing disappointment. They sent me messages, thanking me for being so open. But, honestly, it was them who got me through.

Then finally – *finally* – after years of negative tests, that second line appeared.

I was pregnant.

I told everyone. I was euphoric. After years of limbo, we could start dreaming again.

Finally we could get back to focusing on the business, on our relationship, on being a happy family. We went from being consumed by the present, to once again thinking positively about the future. I was pondering whether it would be a boy or a girl, thinking of names I liked. Planning trips we would take. *I let myself imagine it all.* I believed, truly, that this was our time.

Unfortunately, it wasn't.

It all came crashing down one afternoon during a routine scan. The midwife started off chirpy, excited to show us our baby for the first time. But her expression quickly changed as she started scanning. She said, "I'll be right back," and returned with someone else. The two women scanned in complete silence. I watched their faces, recognising *that look* – the one I knew all too well from my own days in healthcare. They prodded harder, measured lots of things and eventually one of them took a deep breath and broke the silence …

"I don't think your pregnancy is going to progress," she told me gently.

"But, there's a heartbeat, right?" I asked optimistically. I knew enough about those grey/black ultrasound splodges to have recognised that.

There was. A flickering heartbeat. But the baby wasn't growing as expected. I optimistically explained that this was the case with my first baby too – Leo was always much smaller than he should have been. But she wasn't convinced.

"It's very rare to see a pregnancy like this progress," she said. "But we can't say for certain. Come back in a week."

Rare, but not impossible ... I wasn't too concerned. I felt nauseous, I felt pregnant. Our little baby was inside me, its little heart beating away. Surely they must be mistaken.

A week passed, we went for another scan and, still, its little heart was beating away. But this time they were even more certain. It wasn't growing as expected, but the heartbeat was there ... "Come back in another week," they told me. Yet another week of not knowing.

To cut a long and miserable story short, they were right. I started bleeding. I was hysterical. I think it was then that my brain finally caught up – I was going to lose this baby, and there was nothing I could do. After years of fighting to be in this position, reality hit me that even a positive pregnancy test doesn't mean we will get a baby. We were in the small percentage of people who experience secondary infertility, and then the small percentage who don't get pregnant within three rounds of IVF, and now we were in the unlucky percentage who lose their baby. It all seemed so cruel.

I went for another scan where they explained that my cervix was opening, but there was still a heartbeat. They couldn't give me any medication to "speed things up" until the heartbeat wasn't there anymore. Knowing the baby was still alive and trying somehow made things worse. I would put my hands on my belly and whisper *we've got this, we love you* – to someone I knew I would likely never get to meet. Someone I had already imagined in our lives. I had pictured their face, their laugh, them playing with their big brother. I had already loved them into existence – but they were slipping away. Something in my head was still convincing me it *could* be OK. You read similar stories on forums, where, despite everyone saying there was an issue, it all turned out OK. Maybe this will be us.

But the bleeding got heavier and the cramping started. I knew what was happening, even if I wasn't ready to accept it. I'd read enough to know. I remember sitting on the bathroom floor, clutching my stomach and sobbing so violently I couldn't catch my breath. I eventually passed the pregnancy at home. Something I was grateful for. I was worried about passing it into the toilet without knowing and flushing it away, or the midwives taking it in a swab and putting it in the clinical waste at the hospital. I sat sobbing on the bathroom floor, with this tiny little potential life laid on a pillow of toilet paper. It was devastating. And something I will never forget. Luckily, Leo was at nursery when it happened. I took some red felt from his craft box, cut out a heart and wrapped it in there with a little note. João and I went to a place that is special to us, a beautiful woodland area. We dug a little hole by a tree to put it in, put some flower petals in and covered up our baby. Then we just sat and hugged in silence.

This wasn't just a loss. It was the death of a future. Of a baby I already knew, in that strange way only mums do.

But there is no rest, especially when you are as desperate as we were. So we got straight back to it, as soon as we were allowed. There were many days when I thought, *I can't keep doing this*. Days when posting sunny content online felt absolutely ridiculous, when behind the scenes I was injecting hormones, sobbing into negative pregnancy tests and pretending to be OK for the brand deals that were funding our next round of IVF.

I knew I had to keep going. If I ever made it through to the other side – whether I got to hold another baby in my arms or not – I'd want to be able to look back and think, *You did everything you could*.

Ironically, it was our final and poorest-quality embryo that resulted in me being pregnant again. The one we almost didn't use. The one we almost gave up on.

Eventually, the light started to creep back in.

And that's why I'm sharing all of this. Not because it's easy. Not because I'm "over it". But because if *you* are in that darkness, I want you to know you're not alone. You are seen. You are valid. And you will find your way out.
   It might not look the way you hoped.
   It might take longer than you think.
   But joy will find its way back to you.
   It did for me.
   So if you're still with me, thank you.
   Thank you for witnessing this part of my story.
   It's not easy to share, and it's not easy to read – but I believe in the power of honesty, and I believe in showing the *full* picture, not just the curated highlights.
   Because life doesn't stop when you're struggling. And neither does motherhood. Or work. Or travel.
   Which brings us to Chapter Eight …

Chapter Eight
BUMPS, BAGS AND BABYMOONS

For many people, pregnancy signals the end of spontaneous adventures – but, of course, I see it a little differently. Whether it's a relaxed babymoon or a simple weekend escape before the real chaos begins, travel can be a powerful pause button; a moment to breathe, reflect and actually *enjoy* this fleeting chapter of life. And if you're navigating pregnancy after loss, that space becomes even more important. Anything that helps quieten the spiralling thoughts, even just for a while, is a gift worth giving yourself. You might be waddling through security with snacks stuffed in every pocket, but you're still *you*. And you deserve to treat yourself – and maybe enjoy one last uninterrupted nap by a pool (if you have other children, that might be easier said than done!).

In this chapter, we'll talk about when to travel, how to travel and what to pack when you are triple your usual size. Whether you're six weeks in and feeling green, or six months deep and feeling exhausted – I've got you. Let's make bump travel feel less daunting, more doable and maybe even a little bit fabulous.

THE BEST TIME TO TRAVEL DURING PREGNANCY

Knowing when to travel in pregnancy is difficult, and the best time will likely be different for us all.

First trimester (0–12 weeks)

Here's the deal: a lot of people feel absolutely rubbish during the first trimester – there's nausea, exhaustion, mood swings and that weird can't-put-your-finger-on-it sense of doom that comes with your growing uterus. On top of that, it's considered one of the riskier stages of pregnancy, with miscarriage rates higher in the first trimester.

Some people choose not to travel at all during this time, and that's totally fair (I didn't as I was basically sitting waiting for it to go wrong). If you're clinging to a bag of dry crackers and haven't stayed awake past 7pm in a week, a weekend city break might not hit the way it used to. That said, if you're feeling good and your doctor's on board with it, there's no reason you *can't* travel. Just keep it low-key. This is not the time for jungle hikes or all-you-can-eat sushi cruises. Make sure you know where the nearest healthcare facility with early pregnancy services is. It goes without saying, but make sure you have travel insurance and a copy of your pregnancy notes (either digital or hard copy).

Second trimester (13–27 weeks)

For many women, this is the golden trimester. If you're lucky, your energy returns, your nausea fades and your bump is cute but not yet an obstacle. This makes the second trimester *the* time to travel. In fact, we did all of our international travel in this period.

You still fit comfortably into plane seats, you can walk reasonable distances and you can likely stay awake past dessert. You can do gentle sightseeing, lazy beach days or even a spa break if the treatments are pregnancy-safe. Most airlines are fine with flying at this stage without any sort of medical note *(see p180 for more on this)*, and your maternity jeans will still have some breathing room.

Basically, what I'm saying is: if you want a babymoon, *do it now*.

Third trimester (28+ weeks)

Things get a little more complicated now. Physically, you will likely be slowing down. You may be puffy and achy, and the idea of sleeping anywhere without your pregnancy pillow is hell. I actually vacuum-packed my huge pillow and took it to Egypt when I was 27 weeks pregnant!

Many airlines require a doctor's note if you're flying after 28 weeks, and some cut you off completely at around 36. Even trains and ferries sometimes have rules, so *check everything*. Also ask yourself: if I went into early labour here, would I feel safe and supported? If the answer is no, save the trip for another time.

The third trimester is a great time for a staycation though *(see Chapter Six, p122)*. Plan something chilled – maybe not a trip to LEGOLAND® like we did.

> **TOP TIP**
> **Don't be caught out by the small print.**
> Pregnancy on its own isn't classed as a medical condition, so you don't need to declare it on your travel insurance. If you've had complications, though – things like gestational diabetes or high blood pressure – then you do. Always double-check with your insurer (and your midwife).

TIPS FOR SAFE AND COMFORTABLE TRAVEL AT EVERY STAGE

What you need at 14 weeks versus what you need at 34 weeks can be wildly different, so let's break it down. Here's how to make travelling easier no matter where you are in your pregnancy:

Early pregnancy (first and early second trimester)
- **Speak to your midwife before booking:** Even if you're feeling great, get the green light first. This is especially important if you're on any medications or have a previous history of complications.
- **Avoid risky destinations:** Particularly those with a risk of the Zika virus or malaria.
- **Manage the nausea:** If you're still in the "crackers and quiet sobbing" phase, bring whatever helps. For me, that was ginger biscuits, anti-sickness bands and avoiding strong smells (airports are a minefield for this). I remember vomiting in a bin at a bus station when someone opened a bag of Chilli Heatwave Doritos next to me.

- **Pack a "just in case" kit:** Slip a few Ziplock bags and packs of tissues into your bag. If nausea hits suddenly on a bus or in a queue, you'll be *very* glad you're not diving headfirst into a stranger's Pret bag.
- **Include a smell survival kit:** Airports, trains and buses = a sensory minefield. A dab of peppermint oil (or another scent you like) on a hanky can block out the dodgy fast-food smells and help with nausea.
- **Stick to simple travel plans:** Now is not the time to be hopping across three time zones or doing an 18-hour layover in Frankfurt. Short and sweet wins the race.
- **Bring food that you actually want to eat:** Dry cereal, fruit or that one brand of biscuit that you can stomach. Don't rely on airport or service station offerings that may make your stomach turn.
- **Wear comfy, layerable clothing:** Hormones love to mess with your internal thermostat and planes are either ovens or freezers – nothing in between. Make sure you can strip off when needed but maintain some dignity (difficult when pregnant, I know!).
- **Choose aisle seats:** You don't want to clamber over strangers every time you need a wee (which is roughly every 14 minutes).
- **Pace yourself:** Your energy can still be a bit all over the place in early pregnancy. Don't overbook your itinerary. A walk and a nap count as a full day.

Late pregnancy (late second and third trimester)

- **Get a doctor's letter if you're flying:** It's also worth knowing that cruises won't allow you on board after 24 weeks. I learned this the hard way when I was offered a dream job to promote a popular cruise line, just as I hit the 24-week mark. *Gutted.*
- **Consider proximity to healthcare:** You have to think of the worst and imagine you could go into labour there. If so, would you feel safe? Do they have good neonatal care for a premature baby? If not, maybe pick somewhere a little less remote.

- **Move regularly:** This is especially important on long journeys – flex your feet, take aisle strolls and do a little seated ankle rotation dance. Basically, you want to prevent clots, which you are at more risk of while pregnant and immobile.
- **Hydrate:** Bring a giant water bottle and sip from it all day. Yes, you will have to pee 100 times, but you will feel tons better for it.
- **Wear compression socks:** These are great at preventing swelling and blood clots. I had some really funky ones that looked ridiculous in hindsight!
- **Pack your support pillows:** Bring one for your back, under your bump or wherever needs extra love. I took my huge pregnancy pillow *everywhere*!
- **Don't be afraid to ask for help:** From staff, strangers and your partner. You're growing a human. Sit down. Let someone else hoist the bag.
- **Bring easy shoes:** By 30+ weeks, bending down feels like a Cirque du Soleil audition. Slip-on trainers or sandals = dignity saver.
- **Avoid stairs and hilly walks:** If the accommodation says it has "charming elevated views" or "cosy attic rooms", run! (OK, hobble.)
- **Expect to need more rest:** You're carrying a human. You're doing enough.
- **Know your limits:** Be honest with yourself and your partner. If you're tired, stop. If you're uncomfortable, take a break. This is not the time to push through.

Whether you're at the start of the second trimester or nearing the finish line, travelling with a bump just takes a little more planning, patience and a healthy sense of humour!

Safe flying while pregnant

Flying is generally considered safe for most pregnancies, but always double-check with your healthcare provider. Some airlines have strict cut-offs (often 36 weeks for single pregnancies, earlier for multiples), and many require a doctor's letter from 28 weeks onwards. Check their policies before you book – and don't assume the budget airline will be chill about it. If you have a big bump, have some sort of evidence of your gestation. A Ryanair staff member was seriously sus of my gestation when I was only 23 weeks pregnant (I had huge bump problems) so I used my pregnancy tracker app as evidence – luckily, they didn't want anything more official at that point. Also bear in mind:

- Avoid flying if you have certain pregnancy complications. This includes pre-eclampsia, risk of preterm labour or certain placental issues.

PREGNANCY PAMPERING

Before you book spa treatments, ask three things:

1. **Temperature:** Skip hot tubs/saunas/steam rooms and very warm thermal pools. If a pool is >37–38°C (98–101°F), give it a miss.

2. **Positioning:** Make sure you only use pregnancy-trained therapists; only side-lying or raised-back massages after the first trimester, and no deep work on calves/the abdomen.

3. **Ingredients:** Avoid retinoids and high-dose salicylic acid in facials; be cautious with essential oils like clary sage/rosemary.

Pick low-impact wins (float sessions, cool pools) and you'll still get the "pampered" feeling – safely.

- Bring your maternity notes or a summary of your pregnancy history, just in case.
- Opt for destinations with good healthcare access; again, just in case.
- You can skip the scanners at airport security if you want. Though they're usually considered safe for pregnant women and babies, if you're unsure you can ask for a pat-down instead.
- If you're prone to nausea, pop on some travel sickness bands and try ginger sweets. Have a sick bag ready. And maybe don't sit too near the toilets. Oh, and bring *all* the antacids.

Avoiding food poisoning

Your risk of food poisoning is higher during pregnancy, and the consequences can be more serious. So, while I'm normally all for trying local delicacies and saying yes to that questionably grilled street sausage, during pregnancy I'm much more careful.

- Avoid anything raw or undercooked (for example, sushi, rare meat or soft-boiled eggs).
- Stick to bottled or filtered water in countries where the tap water isn't safe to drink. Avoid ice cubes that could have been made with tap water.
- Be careful with salads and fruit that may have been washed in unsafe tap water or touched with dirty hands – peel it yourself if you're unsure.
- Avoid unpasteurised cheeses, deli meats and buffet food that looks like it's been sitting out since breakfast.
- Wash your hands often – especially after handling money. Notes and coins are basically Petri dishes in your pocket.

WHAT TO PACK WHEN YOU'RE PREGNANT

Packing is always one of my less enjoyable travel tasks – throwing in a bump adds an extra layer of *fun*. (Why is it not socially acceptable to just swan about in a giant shawl all week?) Here are the essentials:

The non-negotiables

- **Maternity notes or a doctor's letter, if applicable:** I've mentioned this what feels like 100 times now, but it's so important to pack so I'm saying it again here. Keep them in your hand luggage – not packed under five layers of swimwear. Like me, you might find yourself having to prove your huge bump isn't quite ready to pop.
- **Any medications or supplements:** Pregnancy vitamins, antacids, pain relief, anti-nausea meds, and anything your midwife's told you not to miss. Pack more than you think you'll need. Antacids were my best friend towards the end of my pregnancy.
- **Refillable water bottle:** I had a bottle that filters water as you drink it, which gave me peace of mind and meant I could fill up anywhere.
- **Compression socks:** These are not glamorous, but neither are cankles. Pick jazzy patterns if it makes you feel better about life.
- **Comfy shoes:** Preferably ones that slip on and off easily and don't constrict your elephant feet.
- **Loose, breathable clothing:** Anything that doesn't dig in, rub or ride up. Think soft fabrics and forgiving waistbands. Bonus points for anything that doubles as PJs.
- **Eye mask and earplugs:** Use them shamelessly. It may be the last chance you get for undisturbed sleep in the next five years.
- **Sanitary pads or panty liners:** If you know, you know.
- **Spare underwear in hand luggage:** On a similar note, pregnancy is full of surprises, and not the good kind.

The nice-to-haves

- **Cooling spray and/or handheld fan:** You can thank me later.
- **Belly support band:** Glamorous it is not, but your lower back will thank you after a day of waddling through airports.
- **Mini first aid kit:** Include plasters, paracetamol, antihistamines and antiseptic wipes.

- **Entertainment:** Think audiobooks, podcasts, your Kindle – something to get you through the hours when you're too bloated to nap but too knackered to speak.
- **An oversized scarf or wrap:** This can act as a blanket, makeshift pillow or emergency outfit if you spill something down you (which you will). I had a giant poncho that made me look like Homer Simpson in his "muumuu era" – niche reference, but it was *so* comfy.
- **Small day bag or backpack:** For all the *just in case* extras you'll accumulate. Give it to someone else to carry, of course.

Packing while pregnant isn't about being Pinterest-perfect – it's about survival, comfort and being prepared for anything your hormones (or Ryanair) throw at you. Keep it simple, practical and forgiving.

Travelling while pregnant isn't always easy, but it *is* possible – and it can be wonderful. Whether it's your first baby or your fifth, there's something special about carving out space to connect, slow down and celebrate the carnage that's coming. Say yes to naps. Say yes to dessert. Say yes to a little adventure before the next one begins. You've earned it.

Now, let's talk about what happens when that bump turns into a baby …

PLANNING THE PERFECT BABYMOON

Here are my top tips for nailing the babymoon vibe:

- **Pick somewhere you'll actually nap:** That "boutique hotel above a lively tapas bar" sounds cute until you're up at 2am with heartburn and someone's singing "Despacito" beneath your window. Look for peace and quiet over "Instagrammable chaos".

- **Check the bed reviews:** A lumpy mattress at 30 weeks pregnant is essentially torture. Scan reviews for words like "firm", "comfortable" or "cloud-like". Avoid anywhere with "rustic charm" = code for "back pain guaranteed".

- **Avoid long-haul flights if you can:** These aren't fun at the best of times. Keep it short, keep it comfy, keep yourself sane.

- **Book flexible dining:** Pregnancy cravings and aversions change daily. Buffet or all-day dining means you're not locked into an 8pm five-course tasting menu when all you actually want is chips at 4pm before going to bed.

- **Always get air con:** Late pregnancy = your own personal central heating system. Don't scrimp here. A fan won't cut it when you're heavily pregnant and sweating through a linen maxi dress.

- **Avoid remote destinations with poor access to medical care:** If something goes wrong, you want to be able to get help quickly.

- **Check for Zika virus risks:** Check the NHS or CDC travel advice before booking.

- **Book somewhere with a pool:** Floating = weightless pregnancy bliss.

- **Find spas that cater to pregnancy:** Many offer maternity-safe massages, facials and pampering, which is exactly what you need.
- **Don't over-schedule:** The plan is *rest*, not "fit in every possible activity before your pelvic floor gives up".
- **Plan a mini photoshoot:** Even if you feel puffy and yuk, you'll want the memories. Get your partner to snap a few nice photos in good light – and don't delete them! You'll treasure them later when you're knee-deep in nappies.

MANAGING PREGNANCY SYMPTOMS ON THE ROAD

Travelling while pregnant is rarely glamorous. One minute you're glowing, floating in a pool and feeling like a goddess. The next you're sweaty, bloated and hobbling to the loo for the 33rd time that day. Some days, it's a babymoon. Other days, it feels like you packed for a spa break and ended up on a budget survival show.

The trick? Plan ahead. The roughest days I had were when I wasn't prepared – trying to fight nausea without snacks, heartburn without antacids or bad sleep without my trusty pillow. Your "pregnancy kit" will make or break your trip. Here's how to survive the common culprits:

Nausea
- Eat small, regular meals (graze like a farm animal).
- Pack mints, ginger biscuits or *your* magic food.
- Avoid strong smells (airports are one giant smell roulette you didn't sign up for).
- Sickness bands or behind-the-ear patches helped me.
- Set *clear* food boundaries: threaten violence if your partner even *thinks* about opening a tin of tuna.

Fatigue
- Rest when you need to.

- Schedule lazy mornings and guilt-free naps.
- If you wake up and feel like today's itinerary is "lie down and eat", that's valid. You're growing a human – you're the boss of this trip. One of my best pregnancy memories was relaxing on a Bali bed by the sea having fresh fruit and cold drinks delivered to me like the queen I was.

Heartburn
- It's all about the antacids: pack them, hoard them, worship them. You can't take too many.
- Eat earlier in the evening so food has time to leave your stomach before you lie down.
- Skip the spicy buffet (I know, cruel).

Overheating
- Avoid the midday sun – you're already running your own internal furnace.
- Stick to loose, light clothes.
- Dip your feet in the pool/fountain/any water source that won't get you arrested.
- Handheld fan and spray bottles = the MVPs of late-pregnancy travel.

Swelling
- Elevate your feet like the queen you are.
- Wear compression socks (bonus: mosquitoes can't get through them).
- Drink water constantly.
- Pro tip: compression socks double as an excuse not to shave your legs.

Chapter Nine
TRAVELLING WITH A BABY

Your baby arrives, your life is thrown into chaos and travelling somewhere exotic probably isn't top of your to-do list. Totally fair. Travelling with a baby can seem terrifying. Most sane people need a moment (or several hundred) to just come to terms with the fact that there's now a tiny human relying solely on them for *literally everything*. There's also a *lot* to think about: passports, bottle sterilisation and, of course, the fear of being *that* parent with the screaming baby on the plane. (Babies cry; people do get over it.) But, at the same time, there's absolutely no reason parenthood should put your passport into retirement. Not only is travel with a baby *doable*, it can actually be, dare I say it ... enjoyable. I know – bold claim. But stick with me.

Before we get into the tips, let me share how our second baby, Luca, entered the world – it explains a lot about why I believe in *living your life now*, not waiting for the "right" time. Luca made his entrance with a bang. Everything took a turn after a long day out at LEGOLAND®. All day, I had been feeling dizzy, in constant pain and exhausted, but I brushed it off as the price of waddling around a theme park in my unfit state. The next day, I went to a routine antenatal appointment – the kind I almost rescheduled. It quickly turned into anything but routine. I was diagnosed with severe pre-eclampsia: dangerously high blood pressure that put me at serious risk of seizures, organ failure and worse. It's a condition that can become life-threatening for both mum and baby, and I was admitted to hospital, where I needed high-dependency monitoring. It was one of those situations where you look back and think: LEGOLAND® in that state was probably not my finest idea. But it taught me a lot – about asking for help, not pushing through when you shouldn't and about how little support there is for pregnant travellers.

Luca wasn't due for another six weeks, so the goal was to keep him cooking for as long as possible without compromising my health. Pre-eclampsia can only be resolved once the baby is born – which means it's always a balancing act: wait too long and the mum suffers; deliver too early and the baby might experience problems. I didn't mind the hospital stay. To be honest, I'd been braced for something to go wrong the whole pregnancy, so, when it did, I almost felt calmer. At least it was diagnosed, at least there was a plan; sometimes the anticipation is the worst bit.

We made it through a week before things took another turn. My kidneys started to struggle, I was dangerously swollen, my urine output dropped and my blood pressure couldn't be controlled. I was retaining fluid in all the wrong places. It was time.

I was rushed for an emergency C-section.

Luckily, Luca was a whopper for 35 weeks – 6 lb (2.7 kg) – and healthy, thanks to the steroid injections I was given that helped his lungs develop early. Fortunately, he didn't need any time in special care, which I had been really worried about given he was premature.

I lost a lot of blood during the C-section, something called a massive obstetric haemorrhage (MOH). It was a really traumatic experience for me as I heard a panicked shout saying, "Put out a MOH call" (basically a "crash call" for when a delivering mum is bleeding a lot). Tons of people then rushed into the operating theatre, they ushered João away from my side and I was listening as they discussed how there was 2.5 L (0.5 gal) of blood in the suction already (half my blood volume), and that the bleeding wasn't stopping. Having the surgical knowledge that I have, I knew things weren't good.

I was dipping in and out of consciousness as I looked across to my perfect little baby. I genuinely believed I was going to die in that moment. I *knew* something was going to go wrong, and this was it. I thought my body had been through too much for me to survive that blood loss. But the baby was out, and safe, and, at the time, that's all that mattered. The next thing I knew, I was in the recovery ward, my tiny baby laid across my chest, his little mouth rooting around for my nipple. I had lots of wires attached to me and dried blood splashed on my arms, but I was OK. I had been dreaming of this moment for years and, despite it not happening how I'd imagined, it was perfect.

Within eight weeks, after a prolonged hospital stay, we would find ourselves in France on Luca's first trip abroad. Because life is too fickle – too fragile – to not get out there and do the things that matter. That first holiday wasn't exactly smooth sailing – there were lessons, mistakes and tears (some of them mine) – but it was the beginning of a new chapter. One that confirmed that babies don't have to be the end of your adventures. In fact, they can be the start of even better ones. If you still need convincing, here are five good reasons to travel with your baby:

1. **It's cheap:** Most under-twos fly for a small additional fee, they often eat free and sleep for free. It's basically the golden window before you have to start paying for them.
2. **They can't run away, yet:** Babies stay where you put them. Enjoy it while it lasts.
3. **They love new sights:** Whether it's a beach, a tree or a spoon they've not seen before, babies are fascinated. Everything is new and wonderful to them. You don't need expensive excursions or attractions – their highlight might just be a hotel ceiling fan.
4. **Family memories:** Sure, they won't remember their first dip in the sea, but you will. Those early adventures are the photos you'll look back on when they're teenagers rolling their eyes at you. I hate the "they won't remember it" comment – we get it a lot. No one remembers learning to walk, or read, or speak, but it was still important!
5. **Maternity leave:** No annual leave request needed. You're already off work, so why not swap your living room for a sun lounger (with the same amount of laundry, but a better view)?

In this chapter, I'm going to break it all down – planning, packing, flying, feeding; the good, the bad, the leaky nappies, and everything in between. Travelling with a baby is different, but it doesn't have to be difficult.

PLANNING BABY'S FIRST TRIP

Before we get to the super cute baby-on-a-beach pics, let's deal with the not-so-fun admin bits. You can't exactly pop a baby in your carry-on and hope for the best (although wouldn't that be so much easier?). Here is my checklist when you're planning your baby's first holiday:

- **Get the birth certificate:** Applying for a baby passport, and pretty much anything official, requires a birth certificate. Appointments to register your baby – and get the birth certificate – can be limited, so consider the time needed to get this, and then the time needed to apply for the passport itself. Being able to jet off within a few weeks of the birth is likely very optimistic.
- **Take the passport photo:** Ever tried getting a newborn to look at the camera, eyes open, mouth closed, not smiling, not frowning and not slumping over like a drunk uncle at Christmas? Good luck. Luckily, the authorities are quite lax with newborn photos. My tip? Do it when they're just fed and slightly sleepy. We put one of those "flat head" donut pillows under a white sheet. It kept his head facing forward and provided a nice plain background.
- **Apply for the passport:** Unless you enjoy stress and queues at the passport office, give yourself some time. In the UK, it usually takes a few weeks for a passport to arrive, but it's wise to allow up to ten. You can get a faster appointment (for a price). We paid for a one-week fast-track service to make sure we got it in time.
- **Check vaccinations:** Check what vaccines your baby will have had by the time you want to travel. Some destinations require additional jabs, so plan around that. If you're flying before their routine jabs, discuss it with your GP or travel nurse to assess for any risks.

IDEAL DESTINATIONS AND ACCOMMODATIONS

As you know, our first trip with Leo was to Portugal to see João's family. He was six weeks old. It was a short flight (Leo – and I – slept through it all), my parents came too (extra hands) and staying with family meant we had all the miscellaneous baby kit we could wish for.

A NOTE TO SOLO PARENT TRAVELLERS

If you're flying solo (you absolute legend), it's even more important to plan ahead. Book airport assistance if it is available, make use of baby-wearing and pack light (yes, really). You don't need 15 muslins and a stash of nappies for the entire trip. You can buy things when you get there. You need your hands free and your patience intact.

Our first trip with Luca was to a Center Parcs in France when he was eight weeks old. We drove there (so we could throw everything in the car), we requested everything from a cot to a baby bath and we planned very little for the time we were there. Having minimal plans meant we could take each day as it came. Some days were more active than others, but there was no pressure to do more than we were comfortable with. Driving with a young baby can be tedious – NHS guidance advises that they shouldn't be in a car seat for longer than two hours at a time. I sat in the back to keep an eye on him and we stopped the car to get him out – a lot!

Choosing a destination

Choosing the right destination is more important than ever when travelling with a baby. My advice is to choose somewhere "easy" for your first trip. This is not the time to go backpacking through the Andes. Think: nearby cities with good healthcare, family-friendly resorts or coastal towns with lots of shade and chilled-out vibes. When picking where to go, consider the following:

- **The climate:** Too hot? Never a good idea with a little temperature-sensitive human. Too cold? Layering up a wriggling baby is like wrestling an octopus into a snowsuit. Go Goldilocks on this one: not too hot, not too cold, but just right.
- **If it's pram-friendly:** Cobbled streets look nice on Instagram, but they're no fun on pram wheels – unless you have a pram with those huge inflatable tyres; in which case, you should be OK. If you're heading somewhere hilly or historic, consider a decent baby carrier. It's also a great workout, which won't do us any harm.
- **Access to medical care:** No one likes to think about hospitals when planning a holiday, but it's important. Make sure your destination has easy access to medical care, just in case.
- **Your baby's age:** A newborn is portable, sleeps a lot and doesn't care where you are. A ten-month-old who's crawling and trying to eat sand? Slightly more complex. On a recent trip, I found Luca chewing on a moth that was only half dead when I retrieved it ... These second babies are *wild*. Factor their development stage into your plans. We have found the hardest time to travel is when they are just becoming mobile. Do you let them crawl all over the dirty airport floor? Or do you spend an hour wrestling a crazed mini pig to stay on your lap because they *must* explore the bin area at Gate 32? I know what I do.

> **TOP TIP**
> **Don't forget travel insurance.**
> It needs to cover your baby too. Always be honest when filling out your policy. Yes, previous medical conditions might bump up the price, but if you leave anything out they could refuse to pay out when it matters most.

Choosing accommodation

Choosing the right accommodation when you have a baby is important. Favour family-friendly hotels, aparthotels or self-catering over ultra-luxe honeymoon hideaways – no one wants death stares at

breakfast after a 7am nappy blowout. Here are some things to think about when planning your trip:
- **Sleep setup:** Request a cot in advance (if your baby will sleep in it). Ask if they have blackout curtains. A one-bed apartment or studio with a sliding door = adult evenings back. If it has a balcony with a nice view to enjoy with a bottle of wine, that is priceless.
- **Kitchen bits:** A kitchenette (kettle, microwave, hob, fridge/freezer box) makes bottles, purées and snacks easy. Bonus points for a dishwasher and washing machine. Unfortunately, mess resolution is now part of your life.
- **Baby-friendly facilities:** A shaded baby pool or splash pad, high chairs in the restaurant and an on-site mini-market save you hauling gear. Some family resorts offer bottle warmers, sterilisers, baby baths and changing mats on request – always ask.
- **Location, location:** Think flat terrain, lifts and ramp access for the buggy. And check whether it is close to a supermarket, pharmacy and playground. A ground-floor room or a big balcony/terrace is gold for nap times.
- **Room safety:** Check balcony railings, move breakables up high and inspect the cot (you're looking for a firm mattress with a tight fit). If you're travelling somewhere tropical, ask about mosquito nets or screened windows.
- **Noise and naps:** Choose rooms away from bars/entertainment and pool pumps. If a property has nightly shows, request a room on the quieter wing.
- **Policy check:** Many places let under-twos stay free and provide cots, but some charge – confirm cot availability, fees and late checkout options before you book.

FLYING WITH A BABY

This is the bit that strikes fear into the hearts of many. But flying with a baby isn't the horror show it's made out to be. You just need to be prepared.

Check-in allowances

Most airlines let you bring a pram and a car seat for free – check with the airline before travelling. We make the most of this allowance by using a car seat bag; we put the car seat into a car seat travel bag, we then strap a rucksack to the car seat filled with all the baby's bits. We also put our big liquids in here when travelling with hand luggage only. Free check-in bag = winning. (This is not official advice, just what we do!)

Boarding the plane

Some say board first for extra time. I say board last so you spend the least amount of time on the plane as possible. Sitting in a cramped seat with a wriggly baby for 40 extra minutes while everyone else boards? No thanks. I want to be the very last person on and the first person off.

Where to sit

We like to sit at the back of the plane. It means we can easily board last and, if they open the rear doors, we're first off too. In our experience, most parents have the same idea, so the back tends to be the more "baby-tolerant" zone. The front of the plane can have bulkhead seats with bassinets (more on those in a sec), but otherwise it's often filled with people who still expect some peace and silence.

> **TOP TIP**
> **Be prepared for blowouts.**
> Bring two changes of clothes for baby and one for you. Yes, *you*.
> Because if they poo up their back during take-off, guess who's catching the fallout? (Been there!)

Lap infant versus own seat

Under-twos fly as a lap infant for a small additional fee. This basically means they sit on your lap and don't have their own seat. But if you can afford the extra seat, consider it – especially on long haul. We have an inflatable bed that we use often when flying overnight or a longer distance. Not all airlines allow them, but we have found that most do (Emirates was one airline we flew with that absolutely was

PACKING LIST FOR BABY'S FIRST HOLIDAY

- [ ] Passport
- [ ] Nappies (enough for a few days, plus travel)
- [ ] Biodegradable wet wipes and nappy bags
- [ ] Travel changing mat
- [ ] Bottles, steriliser tablets/bags
- [ ] Formula and/or breastfeeding supplies
- [ ] Calpol, teething gel, thermometer
- [ ] Baby sun cream and sunhat
- [ ] Baby sunglasses for cute photos
- [ ] Lightweight pram or carrier
- [ ] Baby clothes (x2 changes per day)
- [ ] Ziplock bags (for dirty clothes, half-eaten snacks, used wet wipes – trust me, they're heroes)
- [ ] Swimsuit, swim nappies
- [ ] Blanket or muslins
- [ ] Baby monitor (if you're in an apartment)
- [ ] Toys, books, blankets
- [ ] Baby wash, shampoo and a flannel
- [ ] Snacks and pouches (if weaning)
- [ ] Dummy (plus spares – very important!)
- [ ] Sling or baby carrier
- [ ] First aid kit
- [ ] Noise machine or white noise app if you use one
- [ ] Clip-on pram fan (for warm destinations – lifesaver during naps)
- [ ] SnoozeShade
- [ ] Baby swim float or ring (if you're planning on spending time in the water)

not having it). Our dream setup is having a bassinet for the baby and the inflatable for our older child. He used it right up to age five. Remember, you have zero chance of a peaceful flight unless the kids are asleep.

Feeding and ears
Feed during take-off and landing to help with ear pressure. Breast, bottle or dummy all work. If your baby refuses to eat, do not panic – they'll survive; you can only try your best.

Bassinets
On long-haul flights, ask for a bassinet seat when booking. These things are magic. You get extra legroom, and baby gets their own little bed – everyone wins. That said, booking one is often easier said than done. Many airlines will tell you they can't guarantee it and, in our experience, they mean it. We flew to Japan with Air China, requested a bassinet and ended up smack in the middle of the plane – while the entire bulkhead rows (where the bassinets go) were full of baby-free passengers. And nope, no one fancied swapping. When it works, it's brilliant. But for your own sanity, maybe accept that you may end up being the bassinet.

ON-THE-GO BABY CARE
Looking after your baby while travelling isn't actually that different from looking after them in your living room – except now you've got better scenery and probably worse Wi-Fi. Babies are simple creatures: feed them, keep them comfy, keep them close, and nine times out of ten you'll have a happy travel buddy (the tenth time, nothing will work and you'll just have to ride it out – sorry). The key is being prepared.

Transport planning
When it comes to getting around, think simple and safe. If you're hiring a car, bring your own car seat. Rental ones are often expensive, questionably clean and occasionally look like they've survived a small

explosion. On public transport, babies usually travel free – and you'll be surprised how many strangers turn into your personal assistants the second you're juggling a pram, a baby and 14 bags of "essentials". A lightweight travel buggy is amazing for quick folds and narrow doorways, but a comfy baby carrier is just as handy. Think of it as strapping a hot water bottle to your chest that occasionally screams, but it frees up your hands and makes cobbled streets or endless stairs a lot less stressful.

Routine management
Some babies thrive on routine; others love chaos. Try to keep a *rough* sleep/feed schedule, but don't stress. A later bedtime in the sunshine won't ruin them forever. Bring a carry cot or pram that lies flat for tiny babies – they will hopefully happily snooze in there while you enjoy your evening meal out. For what it's worth, we've never been strict with routines and our kids are now brilliantly adaptable.

Mini first aid kit
Include Calpol, teething gel, a thermometer, plasters, hand sanitiser and a toy or two to occupy them when they're about to kick off.

Bottle-feeding
Lots of parents panic about how on earth they'll sterilise bottles on holiday – but, honestly, it's much easier than you think. Pack sterilising tablets or a microwave steriliser bag if you know you'll have access to a microwave. Personally, we prefer the cold-water method: a good hot soapy wash first, then into sterilising solution. A collapsible bucket is a genius addition if you're worried the hotel sink or bath won't cut it.

When it comes to formula, most hotels will happily supply a kettle so you can boil water. Ready-made cartons are absolute lifesavers for travel days – no faff, no waiting, no meltdown in the departure lounge. We never even bother warming them; Luca quickly adapted to room-temperature milk. If your baby insists on it being warm (like Leo did), bring a flask of boiling water and some pre-measured formula containers. That way, you can make a bottle on the go, then use a rapid-cool flask or a bowl of cold water to get it down to a safe temperature quickly. With Leo, we'd often prep a bottle about half an hour before boarding, let it cool naturally and have it ready for take-off.

CRUISING WITH A BABY

Cruising with Luca when he was 15 months old was one of our most relaxing family trips. We hopped between new places with all the comforts of the ship and it was far better than we'd imagined. Here are a few quick tips if you're planning a cruise holiday with tiny ones:

- **Smart booking:** Choose lines with a nursery or under-three club, guarantee a travel cot and pick a midship, lower deck cabin for less motion. Some cruise lines are more family-friendly than others, so read up before booking.
- **Sleep:** Luca slept amazingly on our cruise. Probably because he could feel the gentle rocking and low hum of the ship. Book an inside cabin – it will be totally dark at night, cheaper than a balcony cabin and you don't have to worry about a mobile child trying to scale the balcony barrier!
- **Feeding and bottles:** Check there will be a kettle and mini-fridge for hot water and storing purées. Pack pouches, bibs, spoons and sterilising tablets. Crew can warm milk – just ask.
- **Pools reality check:** Most lines don't allow non-toilet-trained babies in pools. Look for splash pads and pack a small inflatable tub for "bath time" in the shower. We saw one family with a small paddling pool next to their sunbeds on the deck – genius!
- **Shore days:** Favour pram-friendly ports; tender ports (ones where you need to get a smaller boat to shore) can be a

faff. Keep naps flexible and aim to be back on board before the meltdown window. We only spent a few hours at each port, and that was enough for us all.

- **Routines and sanity:** Book early dining slots, use room-service breakfast (if available) and reserve nursery slots on embarkation day.
- **Health and safety:** Check the minimum age rules (often 6–12 months on some routes), confirm they provide infant life jackets, pack medicines and a thermometer and get travel insurance that covers cruises.
- **Never leave your baby unattended:** If you want adult time, use the ship's nursery/babysitting where offered – don't rely on monitors outside your cabin port.

Capture the memories

Take *all* the photos – even the ones where they're mid-meltdown. Their first swim, their first paddle, that confused "What is this?" face on their first flight; it's all part of the story. Whether it ends up in a baby book or just buried in your overflowing camera roll, you'll be so glad you captured it. With both of our boys, I still look back and think, "I wish we'd taken more" – and we literally have thousands.

Travelling with a baby is not only possible, it can be really fun. It's messy, chaotic and full of surprises, but it's also magical and the memories will stick with you forever. You'll feel braver, stronger and more resourceful than you ever thought possible. And when you're sitting on the beach, your baby asleep on your chest, you'll think, "Yeah, it was worth it." Now go book that trip! You've got this.

Babies are portable and relatively easy to travel with. Little kids? Not so much. They run, they shout, they demand the most ridiculous things – and yet, travelling with them opens up a whole new world of adventure. The next chapter is all about surviving – and actually enjoying – travel with little kids.

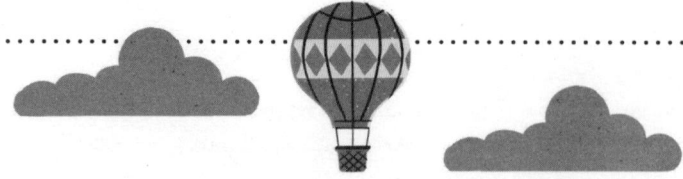

LESSONS LEARNED

Let's talk about some disasters and near-misses we have had while travelling with babies, because they're inevitable and maybe you can learn from them!

Visa panic
We booked a once-in-a-lifetime trip to Florida when Leo was ten months old. We got to the airport and realised we had applied for an ESTA (an online travel authorisation you need to travel visa-free to the USA) for everyone but Leo. We were incredibly lucky to apply for one there and then and have it approved just before check-in closed!

Nappy catastrophes
One memorable flight included a code-brown incident at the start of take-off. No nappy changes allowed, no escape. We sat marinating in poo for 20 minutes, and it stank. It exploded out of his nappy, soaked through his cute little romper and was caught by my cream trousers … Glorious. As I've said, always, always pack spare everything, for everyone.

Security shenanigans
Going through security with bottles, breast milk and a buggy? Not fun. Arrive early and be patient. The security

staff really don't care that your baby's screaming – they will test every single bottle of your milk like it's a chemical weapon. I recently made the rookie error of packing 15 pouches of puréed food in my carry-on. Security pulled me aside like I was smuggling uranium. There's nothing like explaining to a stony-faced official why you need half a kilo of puréed sweet potato to survive a two-hour Ryanair flight.

Expensive check-in

While we were in the midst of our fertility struggles, we did something we are constantly advising people to avoid: we forgot to check in online in advance (certain budget airlines insist on this). I blamed João, and he blamed me. Online check-in had closed and so our only option was to go to the check-in desk with our tails between our legs. The check-in man pulled on his balaclava and charged us £55 each to be handed a flimsy bit of paper with a gate number on it – £165 for the three of us to be able to board our £30 flights! Absolutely wild. Not all airlines do this, but be aware of the ones that do. Forgetting to check in online can potentially rinse your "Whoops Fund" *(p32)*. It's an expensive mistake that we won't ever make again.

Chapter Ten
TRAVELLING WITH LITTLE KIDS

Travelling with babies is easy. Travelling with toddlers and pre-schoolers ... now that sounds brave, right? You're probably picturing tantrums in airport queues, emergency dashes to questionable public toilets and the stubborn refusal to eat anything that isn't beige. And you wouldn't be wrong. But here's the thing: travelling with little kids can also be amazing. Sure, it's messy and occasionally chaotic, but it's also wide-eyed, joy-filled and completely unforgettable.

I still remember our first ferry trip with Leo as a toddler. It was full-on – snacks flying, bags everywhere, mild overstimulation – but then he stepped out onto the deck and saw the open sea, the wind blowing his curls, and his little face just lit up. That moment? Worth the mayhem.

So, before you write off travelling with toddlers as an extreme sport, give it a chance. This chapter is your survival guide: how to do it well, stay (mostly) sane and maybe even enjoy yourself along the way.

WHY TRAVEL WITH LITTLE KIDS?

You'll never see the world in the same way again once you see it through the eyes of a small child. Everything is new to them – and their wonder is contagious. The things they come out with and the questions they ask will leave you laughing for years.

Little kids are natural explorers. Everything is exciting – the sand feels weird, the ice cream tastes different and the pigeons are *fascinating*. They notice things we don't, and they make you slow down and appreciate the little things. (Sometimes because they're lying on the floor refusing to walk – but still, you've slowed down.)

Travelling gently expands their little world. Different languages, foods, landscapes and ways of life spark curiosity, and plant the early seeds of empathy. Your three-year-old might not grasp the concept of global cultures just yet, but they *will* remember the kind waiter who gave them extra breadsticks or the bus driver who smiled and said, "Hola." They start to notice that while people may look, speak or live differently, deep down we're all the same – we all have families, friends, dreams ... and most people, wherever you go, are kind, welcoming and helpful.

Even the simple parts of travel – waiting in line, packing their own little backpack, trying a new food – help build resilience and flexibility. It's hands-on learning, minus the worksheets. There is no better education than experiencing the world, in my opinion.

CHOOSING THE RIGHT DESTINATION FOR LITTLE KIDS

When it comes to travelling with little kids, especially school-aged kids, the destination isn't usually as important as the cost (school holiday prices can be *wild*, and we will come on to that shortly). But *where* you stay within your chosen destination can really make or break your trip. Always opt for space and practicalities over the "wow" factor. Here are a few tips for choosing the right spot with little kids:

- **Accommodation matters:** Opt for places with space to move and for the kids to go wild (think apartments, villas, aparthotels), plus easy access to amenities such as playgrounds, kid-friendly restaurants or a fridge for snacks. A ground-floor apartment with a fenced-off terrace beats a cramped hotel room with a sixth-storey balcony of doom.
- **Think about the evenings:** Have a think about what you will do when the kids are in bed. If you are all based in one small hotel room, with no outside space, you might find yourself going to bed with them! A separate bedroom and/or outside space will mean you can continue your evenings in peace.
- **Match the trip to your child's current obsessions:** Leo once saw the Eiffel Tower on *Peppa Pig* and became completely obsessed,

so when we finally got the chance to visit Paris, his first stop *had* to be climbing the Eiffel Tower. It was one of our favourite city trips because *he* was excited. If your kid's into *Bluey*, Australia suddenly sounds like a great idea. *Moana*? Somewhere with sand and palm trees. Paddington Bear? Time for a trip to London to see Buckingham Palace. Let them lead sometimes – it keeps them engaged and gives your holiday more excitement.

PREPARING FOR A TRIP WITH LITTLE KIDS

With little kids, the build-up can be just as magical as the getaway itself. Once they realise something exciting is coming, the anticipation is half the fun (and sometimes the only thing getting you through the packing). The more you involve them, the smoother the whole adventure will be.

Get them involved

Show them photos of your destination, read books or watch videos together so they know what to expect. This is especially helpful for neurodiverse children, who often thrive on structure and predictability. Bonus tip: if there's a film, cartoon or story linked to where you're going, use it. Heading to Paris? *Ratatouille*. Off to the beach? *Moana*. There's nothing like Disney doing your prep work for you.

Build excitement

A countdown calendar is simple but surprisingly effective. Each day they tick off gets them closer to take-off – and it helps channel that endless "Is it today yet?" energy into something visual.

Pack together

Let them help with packing. Yes, you'll probably have to quietly repack it all after bedtime (no, they don't need 12 teddies and a pirate hat), but giving them some ownership makes them feel involved and in control. Even choosing their travel snacks or the pyjamas they'll wear on the first night away can make the trip feel like *their* big adventure too.

NAVIGATING SCHOOL HOLIDAYS

School-holiday price hikes are a huge bugbear for many parents. Holiday prices often double, and then some, when the kids are off school. In the UK, we are threatened with fines if we travel in term time, which can put families in a difficult position financially. Here are some smart, above-board ways to save during school breaks:

Best times to travel

The August school holidays, Christmas and (bizarrely) the October half term are usually the most expensive times to travel. If you're tied to school holiday dates, look at Easter or the May half term – they tend to offer better value without sacrificing sunshine or sanity. Some regions will have slightly different school holiday dates to the rest of the country, so make the most of those!

The great school fine dilemma (in the UK)

If your child's in a UK state school, missing school for a holiday can come with a hefty fine – and a side of parent guilt. But before you panic, it's worth knowing the rules (and the loopholes).

In most areas, fines only kick in after five *consecutive* days of absence. That means if you head off one or two days before the official holidays begin, you're technically in the clear. End-of-term days are often spent watching films or playing games anyway, so your child likely won't miss anything vital ... except maybe a dodgy DVD from 1996.

And here's another useful thing to be aware of: if your child is under five, you *can't* be fined at all. So take advantage while you can – the savings on flights and accommodation can be huge.

Ditch the beach

When you look at flight prices for the peak school holiday periods, you will notice a huge jump in the price to popular beach destinations when compared to city breaks. A flight from the UK to the island of Mallorca will be much more expensive than a flight to the city of Milan. From Milan, you could travel to Lake Como or Lake Garda, and find a holiday camp that will have entertainment and lots for the kids. City breaks can be great for families too. Think children's museums, theme parks, zoos and picnics in the park, with no sand stuck in awkward places. *(See p103 for more on entertaining the kids on a city break.)*

Consider DIY booking

Always check prices for booking your flights and hotels separately, and compare that to going through a package provider. Your destination likely won't be basing prices on the UK school holidays, and, as long as their local school holidays don't fall on the same dates, you won't see the same hike in pricing that you see with a package provider.

FLYING WITH LITTLE KIDS

Getting the kids on a plane is the part most parents dread. But it doesn't have to be traumatic. (OK, let's be real, it might be a *bit* traumatic, but you *will* survive. Promise.) To be completely honest, we are lucky that both our kids have been good travellers.

There are definitely some things you can do to make the experience more enjoyable for everyone.

Before take-off

- **Toilet stop = non-negotiable:** If your kids are out of nappies, march them to the loo right before boarding. Even if they *swear* they don't need it – they do. Otherwise, the second the seatbelt sign pings on, they'll suddenly be "absolutely bursting".
- **Let them burn energy:** I know some people think kids should sit quietly at the gate like tiny monks, but honestly? A bit of running around is in *everyone's* best interest. As long as they're not ploughing into strangers, let them tire themselves out before being strapped into a tin can for hours.
- **Pack surprise "presents":** A stash of cheap little toys wrapped up like gifts works wonders. We're talking pound-shop gold:

stickers, mini puzzles, colouring books, modelling dough, tiny animals. The unwrapping itself buys you time, and you can ration them out for maximum leverage: "Finish lunch and you can open the next one." Yes, it's bribery. Yes, it works.
- **Download their favourites:** Do *not* rely on in-flight entertainment. Sometimes it's broken, sometimes it's terrible, sometimes it doesn't even exist. Load up their favourite shows, games and audiobooks in advance, and don't forget kid-friendly headphones. Save this for emergencies – it's your last-resort, nuclear-option parenting weapon.

In the air

- **Snacks, snacks and snacks, then ... more snacks:** The secret is packing things that take ages to eat – think easy-peel clementines, little cracker-cheese-ham sets, or anything fiddly enough to buy you five minutes of peace. A variety is key. No one can stay grumpy when they've got options.
- **A dummy, snack or drink to help relieve the pressure:** Take-off and landing can mess with kids' ears, so always be prepared. For older toddlers, even just sipping from a straw or chewing something works well.
- **Sticker books, magic colouring pads, mini puzzles, word searches, spot-the-difference:** Basically an entire arts-and-crafts aisle in your carry-on. Rotate them like a magician pulling rabbits out of a hat. Novelty buys you time.
- **Blanket, dummy, favourite book, white noise app:** If you're flying during their usual nap, recreate home as best you can. If they do nod off, order yourself a gin and feel smug for ten minutes.
- **Don't panic when things go wrong – because they *will*:** Expect mess, not miracles. Something *will* spill. Apple purée *will* explode. And yes, even when they're out of nappies, wet wipes remain your best friend. Don't panic. Breathe, laugh if you can, and remember: every other parent on board is silently cheering you on.

Packing smarts

- **Lightweight toys that multitask:** Go for toys that earn their suitcase space: a soft toy that doubles as a pillow, a muslin that moonlights as a superhero cape or a toy car that buys you a whole hour of peace.
- **Packing cubes = sanity savers:** One cube per category: nappies in one, snacks in another, clothes in a third. At 2am in a dark hotel room, when you're rummaging like a raccoon, you'll thank yourself.
- **Ziplock bags (the unsung heroes):** Dirty clothes, half-eaten snacks, "mystery wet items" or the *treasures* your kid insists on keeping (yes, even the stinky crab claw they claimed would make a great pet). Ziplocks keep it all contained.
- **Nightlight or mini lamp:** Hotel rooms only seem to offer "pitch-black cave" or "CSI interrogation". A soft nightlight makes bedtime calmer and midnight loo trips less traumatic.
- **Favourite snacks + familiar cup:** Familiar = comfort. New = gamble. We once lost Leo's dinosaur cup and spent an entire morning hunting for a replacement. We eventually found one, in a *different colour* (thankfully, it was acceptable). Lesson learned: always pack a spare.
- **Travel cutlery + toddler bottle:** Don't assume restaurants will have child-sized forks or cups. Bring your own and avoid mealtime meltdowns.
- **Safety wristband:** Add your contact details in case they wander off. Bonus points for extra info like "I have autism" or "I don't speak the language." Obviously, the goal is to not lose them, but just in case you do …
- **Laundry hacks:** A tiny bottle of detergent or a stain-remover pen is a lifesaver. Kids attract dirt like it's their superpower. A quick sink wash = one less outfit sacrificed to spaghetti Bolognese.
- **Suction plates/bowls:** If they're weaning, these buy you precious minutes at the breakfast buffet. Slippery tables + porridge + flailing toddler = carnage.

- **Portable blackout blind or travel curtain clips:** Essential if your little one is light-sensitive and you're trying to trick them into a 7pm bedtime in Spain.

> **TOP TIP**
> **Pack spare clothes in your hand luggage – for *everyone*.**
> You do *not* want to sit through a three-hour flight in trousers soaked with apple juice, milk or worse. If you thought you were out of the danger zone now they're a little bigger, you aren't.

LEARNING ON THE ROAD

Travel is education – the kind they won't get from a workbook or in a classroom. There are tons of opportunities for learning while you are out exploring a new destination.

Here are some ways you can make travel interesting and educational for younger kids:

Nature

Beachcombing, hiking, animal spotting or throwing stones into a lake for an hour straight all count as exploration and play-based learning. Learn about an animal that is native to the area you are visiting. Look at pictures, learn some fun facts, and brownie points if you can see it in the wild. Alternatively, visit a zoo and spend time watching animals native to the region.

Take snakes, for example. Instead of just saying "there are snakes", you could talk about the ladder snake – a species native to Spain, where you're staying. Show your kids some pictures, maybe even go and spot one at a local zoo. Chances are, they'll remember the ladder snake far more vividly than if they'd just read about it in a school book.

Culture and language

Let them try the local food. Leo's favourite food is pizza and pasta – he loved learning about where these came from. Being in Italy – the home of his favourite food – is something that has stuck with him for years and the reason he tells people he loves Italy.

Visit local markets, watch street performers and visit museums with hands-on exhibits. These will all help give a "feel" for the country you are in, and lots of opportunities to chat about the smaller details.

We like to play a game where we have to spot things that we wouldn't see at home – anything from spotting the colourful tiled buildings in Portugal to the fact the electricity cables above the street looked different in Japan. This helps the kids be more observant and actually see what's around them, rather than not taking any notice.

Learn basic phrases together. Your small children shouting "bonjour" at strangers = super cute memories. It sets them up for being interested in language and developing this as they get older. Leo likes to learn how to count to ten in different languages.

History for little kids

Yes, you absolutely *can* teach kids history while you travel! Castles, pirate ships, Roman ruins ... they're ready-made adventures. The trick is turning them into a story or a game. If you show a bit of imagination, they'll dive right in with you.

Let's be honest: wandering around piles of old stones is boring without context – for adults *and* kids. But if you've done a little research beforehand, you can bring those ruins to life. Suddenly, that broken wall isn't just rubble; it's the spot where Roman soldiers once stood guard or where pirates might have hidden treasure. History is way more exciting when it's played out in front of you.

Creativity boost

Bring along some creative bits – travel journals, colouring kits, washable paints or even a cheap disposable camera. Leo loves drawing what he's seen on our travels, and it's become a lovely end-of-day ritual. Ask them to draw their favourite part of the day, then try to guess what on earth it is (spoiler: it's rarely what you think). It sparks some brilliant conversations and gives them space to reflect on what they enjoyed, what was a bit rubbish and what they're excited about tomorrow. Plus, the "art gallery" you'll collect by the end of the trip is absolute gold.

THE FUN STUFF ONLY HAPPENS IF THE PRACTICAL STUFF WORKS

You don't have to be militant with the plan – the best days come from playing it by ear and working to everyone's mood and what they are comfortable with – but there are a few practical tips that make travelling with little kids a bit less tricky.

Routines on the go
Try to keep mealtimes and naps *somewhat* consistent, but don't panic if things slide. Kids are way more adaptable than we give them credit for. Always make sure you plan a calm, easy first day to give everyone time to adjust. The holiday routine may not look like the one you have at home, but keeping things predictable is always good for little kids.

Jetlag survival
Early arrival? Great – keep the first day chill. Go for a walk, have an early dinner and, whatever you do, *don't nap at 4pm with them.* (We've made that mistake many times.) Try your best to stay awake until a reasonable bedtime hour. Otherwise, the kids will be awake at 2am and raring to start the day. If we are travelling long haul, we prefer to arrive at night. There aren't many situations where we all turn up well rested and unable to sleep!

> **Tantrum management**
>
> Tantrums happen – it's all part of the package. They happen at home, in the supermarket and, not surprisingly, on holiday too. The key is having a plan for when they do. For some kids, especially those who are neurodiverse or sensitive to noise, a pair of child-friendly headphones can work wonders for managing sensory overload.
>
> The real trick though? Spotting the signs *before* the meltdown hits. Prevention is better than cute Instagram photos – watch for that glazed look, the fidgeting or the sudden refusal to walk. If they don't want their photo taken, move on. If it looks like it's all getting a bit much, try to stay calm and gently remove them from the noise. Find a quiet corner, squat down to their level and acknowledge how they're feeling.
>
> This happened a lot with Leo when he was younger. What helped him most was knowing he wasn't in trouble – just overstimulated. I'd say something like, "It looks like this is feeling a bit too busy right now. Let's sit here for as long as you need." It obviously didn't always work, but, more often than not, it helped him reset.
>
> Remember: it's not about avoiding every tantrum. It's about helping them feel safe and understood when the world gets a bit loud.

Travelling with little kids isn't just possible – it can be amazing. Yes, there will be meltdowns, mess and moments where you question every decision you've ever made (which would be happening at home too!), but there will also be joy, discovery and memories that last a lifetime. Don't wait until they're "old enough" – they're ready now. And, with a bit of planning, you are too.

Travelling with little ones is chaotic, but at least you're in charge (most of the time ...). Travelling with big kids? A whole different ball game. Opinions, independence and a whole lot of attitude join the trip. In the next chapter, we'll talk about how to make it work.

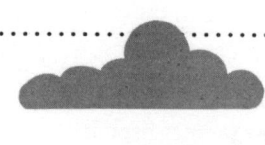

MANAGING PICKY EATERS ABROAD

I know all too well how stressful it is when your child decides they can't eat anything in a new country. We have learned how to work around our sons' picky eating wherever we happen to be – here are the things that have helped us:

- **Pack familiar snacks and a few fruit pouches if they'll eat those:** Do what you've gotta do to get those nutrients in! Leo likes Super Noodles (it has to be the familiar packaging), so we will always pack these as a last resort.
- **Find that familiar meal that you know they will love:** For Leo, it is spaghetti Bolognese or chicken noodles. However, he has some very specific requirements with these. You shouldn't feel awkward asking for things to be prepared how you know they'll eat it. For example, Leo's chicken noodles has to be just that: chicken and noodles. If he glimpses a vegetable in there, he won't eat it. That's not to say he won't eat vegetables – they just have to be familiar and separate to everything else. Again, do what you gotta do.
- **Don't stress if they eat chips for a week:** They won't develop scurvy, promise.

- **Let them help choose from the menu – even if they still end up with plain pasta:** Leo loves to have a look and browse what's on offer, even though I know what he is going to choose (spag bol or bread and butter …). You never know, one day they might surprise you!
- **Choose to self-cater:** All destinations are going to have supermarkets, so you can cook meals you know your picky eater will enjoy.
- **Pack multivitamins:** This will ensure they are still getting the vitamins they need.

Chapter Eleven
TRAVELLING WITH BIG KIDS

We're not at this stage just yet, but I know that travelling with older kids and teens is a whole new ball game. Gone are the days of lugging a buggy through cobbled streets or juggling the logistics of nap schedules. Now, you're navigating mood swings, Wi-Fi demands and whether or not their outfit is Instagram-worthy. But aside from the potential difficulties, it is a fantastic chance to build lasting memories, deepen your connection at a time when they may be drifting and empower them to become confident, curious little(ish) humans. This chapter is all about equipping you to embrace this next phase of family travel. Whether your child is 7 or 17, there are smart ways to involve them, inspire them and give them just the right amount of freedom to thrive.

WHY TRAVEL WITH OLDER KIDS?

Time flies. At the time of writing, my eldest is only six, but time has well and truly *flown*. One minute you're trying to wrestle them into a buggy, the next they're asking if they can download a new game on their iPad. One minute they're laughing at your silly songs and dances, the next they're rolling their eyes. But these middle years are precious. They're old enough to remember the details, to form real opinions and to start seeing the world through a lens that's uniquely theirs.

Family bonding (without eye-rolls)

Older kids still want to connect. Travel gives you the chance to spend real time together without the pressures of school, routines and the same four walls. Away from distractions, you get the best bits of your kids: their humour, their curiosity and their perspective.

Boosting independence

Travelling gives older kids a taste of freedom – and they thrive on it. Whether it's ordering their own food in another language, navigating a foreign city using a maps app or just packing their own suitcase (and forgetting half of what they need), every little experience builds their confidence. Older kids can really get stuck in with the planning stage too. You could even let them choose your hotel if you're feeling brave!

Building real-life skills

Travel teaches older kids things they won't learn in the classroom: how to manage money, handle disappointment, communicate across language barriers and problem-solve in real time. These aren't just travel wins – they're life wins. Give a teen some spending money abroad and, suddenly, you've got a crash course in budgeting. Miss a train? That's resilience training right there. Can't read the menu? Watch them figure out how to point, mime and Google Translate their way to a plate of food. These experiences force kids out of their comfort zone, help them to think on their feet and build confidence in a way textbooks can't. It's a hands-on apprenticeship in "how to adult", with sunshine, ice cream and the occasional dodgy Wi-Fi connection thrown in.

Making the most of these years

This is the time before they potentially start to really pull away. Travel becomes a way to create the kind of memories that actually stick. Years from now, they won't be reminiscing about algebra equations or that worksheet on fronted adverbials – they'll be laughing about the ridiculous family hike where everyone got lost or the time Dad tried to save money on an excursion and you all ended up riding semi-feral horses up a cliff (true story from my childhood!).

It's the little things too – like that tiny bakery in a quiet backstreet in Rome with the most perfect pastries or the evening you all stayed up far too late playing cards in a dodgy Airbnb with questionable plumbing. These become the family stories that get rolled out at Christmas dinners and wedding speeches for decades.

Travel has this magical way of cementing family legends. It gives you inside jokes, shared disasters-turned-adventures and a kind of togetherness you just don't get from sitting silently in the same room scrolling on separate screens.

GET THEM INVOLVED

Older kids are now ready to take a more active role in travel. That doesn't mean handing over the entire itinerary to them, but it *does* mean trusting them with choices and decisions. When they're involved, they're more invested – and a lot less grumpy.

Pre-trip planning
- **Let them pick between a couple of destinations:** They'll love feeling like their vote counts.
- **Get them to do some research:** Ask them to find one activity or sight they'd like to do/see each day.
- **Give them a say in food stops or excursions:** This is democracy in action (with parental veto power).

Packing and organisation
- **Let them pack:** Hand over a packing checklist and leave them to it. You can also do a quick quality-control check at the end to avoid "but I thought three T-shirts was enough for two weeks …".
- **Teach them how to factor in weight limits, essentials and the weather:** It's like real-life Tetris with socks and hoodies.

Money management
- **Give them a daily budget for snacks and souvenirs:** It's budgeting, mental arithmetic and economic heartbreak all in one when they realise £10 doesn't stretch very far in the local currency.
- **Talk through exchange rates:** Help them to understand what's actually good value so they can start spotting the difference between a bargain and a rip-off.

- **Show them how to track spending:** They can use an app or a simple notebook.

Financial literacy is one of the best skills travel can teach and, unlike algebra, they'll actually use it for the rest of their lives.

Assign real tasks
- **Let them find directions to your next stop:** Use Google Maps or an old-school paper map, depending on your vibe.
- **Ask them to book tickets online or at kiosks:** This teaches independence plus tech skills.
- **Encourage them to pick somewhere to eat:** Remind them to factor in budget, distance and everyone's preferences.

When kids are involved like this, travel stops being something that's "done to them" and becomes something they feel part of. It's a sneaky way to build confidence, independence and responsibility – all while making your own life a little easier.

These are all practical skills they'll take into adulthood – plus, you get a bit of a break from being the only one who knows what's going on. Teaching them to not only love travel, but know how to travel sensibly, is a fantastic skill – one that they will use in a few years' time when they are taking you on holiday (she says, hopefully)!

TRAVEL STYLES THAT WORK

The trick to travelling with older kids and teens is to match the trip to their interests and energy levels. Dragging a sulky 14-year-old around an art gallery when they'd rather be surfing? Disaster. But pick the right style of trip and suddenly they're engaged, enthusiastic and even (dare we say it) fun to be around.

City breaks
Cities are buzzing playgrounds for older kids who love food, culture and people-watching. Mix up sightseeing with downtime: one

cathedral visit followed by bubble tea and shopping. Let them help choose the experiences – maybe they'll want to hunt down the best burger joint in Berlin or try a cooking class in Barcelona. Cities are also prime Instagram and TikTok territory, which means they're motivated to get out and explore (bonus points for anything colourful, quirky or "aesthetic").

Adventure travel
If your big kid craves adrenaline, lean into it. Hiking, skiing, kayaking, surfing, canyoning, mountain biking – there's no shortage of ways to keep them buzzing. The key is balance: pack the mornings with thrills, then leave afternoons for naps, Netflix or poolside chilling. Theme parks are also a brilliant option: older kids are finally tall enough for the big rollercoasters and they'll happily lap the park all day while you sneak off for a quiet coffee *(see p134 for my theme park tips)*.

Beach holidays
Sun, sea and sand aren't just for toddlers with buckets and spades. Teens can turn a beach into their own playground: snorkelling, paddleboarding, playing beach volleyball or just flopping with a book and headphones. Beaches also give older kids freedom – they can swim or kick a football about without you hovering round them. For more laid-back kids, this is often the dream: low pressure, lots of space and zero need to fight through crowds like you do in a city.

Slow travel
Staying put for longer lets older kids find their groove. Instead of rushing from one hotel to another, they can actually feel at home in a new place. Think long summer stays in one villa, house swaps or volunteering programmes where they meet other teens. Road trips also work well: they bring variety, but with the comfort of your own "base". Slow travel encourages independence – older kids can wander to the same neighbourhood bakery every morning or be trusted to fetch bread from the corner shop.

LEARNING ON THE ROAD

Older kids are naturally curious, especially when what they're learning feels relevant and interesting. Travel is the best way to bring geography, history, science and culture to life in ways a textbook never could.

History comes alive

History doesn't have to mean dusty old buildings and yawns. When you're standing in the middle of a centuries-old castle or walking through ancient ruins, it suddenly *clicks* – these weren't just people in books, they were real lives, real drama, real sword-fighting chaos.

Castles, ruins, battlefields, old towns – they're all perfect for storytelling. Don't just say, "This is a Roman fort," say, "Imagine being here in full armour, sweating buckets, trying not to get stabbed with a spear." It might not look like it, but they're taking it in.

Find out what they're studying at school (a task in itself, I know) and, if it's Romans, Vikings, World War II or something else, try to work it into the trip. Seeing a topic in real life – the places, the artefacts, the context – can make even the most reluctant learner perk up.

Make it interactive
- **Book a guided tour with a *good* storyteller:** Not the monotone kind, but the ones who make you feel like you're in a Netflix drama.
- **Try an audio guide or walking tour app:** Many are brilliantly done and let you move at your own pace (a win when you've got a sulky teen in tow).
- **Try a VR experience or interactive museum:** Many historic sites offer digital add-ons that bring the past to life brilliantly.

Make it a challenge
- **Ask the kids to be the "family historian" for the day:** They can research the place beforehand and share the best facts. Get them to read the guidebook or guide everyone with the map.
- **Turn it into a photo scavenger hunt:** For example, find a cannon, a gargoyle, something over 500 years old.

History is full of drama – betrayal, invention, revolutions, scandals. It's basically real-life *Game of Thrones* and, when you frame it like that, it suddenly gets a lot more interesting.

Nature and science on the move

Nothing brings science to life like actually seeing it. Forget textbooks and tired PowerPoint slides – the real world is the best classroom there is. Climbing an actual volcano? That's geography, geology *and* adrenaline, all in one sweaty hike. We once visited Timanfaya National Park in Lanzarote. They did experiments like pouring a bucket of water into a hole in the ground, which instantly evaporated with a dramatic "poof!" (it was more exciting than a *poof*, but I can't think of a better description!). They also cooked chicken over the volcano's heat – something Leo still remembers years later.

Exploring caves, national parks or conservation areas? Suddenly, words like "stalactite" and "biodiversity" actually mean something. Aquariums and science museums are a win too – they're hands-on and usually come with air con. Bonus. Plus, they give you a chance to talk about climate change, ecosystems and even space, without sounding like you're lecturing them.

Language and culture

One of the best parts of travelling? Realising the world doesn't all operate like it does back home. New languages, different customs, quirky habits – it's all part of the adventure, and older kids are at the perfect age to soak it up. The key is to start small:

- **Learn a few key phrases together before you go:** Start with "Hello", "Thank you" and "Can I have some ice cream, please?" (arguably the most important). Then actually *use* them in shops, cafés or at the hotel check-in. It can be a bit awkward, sure, but it's also fun – and locals *love* it when kids make the effort. It's confidence-building, character-building and often hilarious.
- **Head to a local market and turn it into a foodie treasure hunt:** What's that weird fruit? How many kinds of bread can we try?

Comparing it all to what you eat at home is a great way to spark curiosity about how people live – and eat – differently.
- **Talk about what you notice:** Is there a traditional dress? Are people quieter or louder than back home? Do people kiss cheeks, bow, wave or just awkwardly nod like us Brits? It's fascinating to see how etiquette and values vary – and it's a brilliant way to open up conversations about respect, tolerance and appreciating difference.

Cultural etiquette and real-world conversations

Older kids are old enough to learn not just *where* they are, but *how* to be there respectfully. Travel is a brilliant way to introduce discussions around cultural norms, global issues and empathy. Here are some ideas to explore with them:
- **Talk about greetings and gestures in other cultures:** What's polite in one place may be offensive in another.
- **Discuss clothing norms:** This is especially important when visiting religious or sacred sites.
- **Share why we try to learn a few words in the local language:** It's not about perfection, it's about respect.
- **Chat about sustainability:** Have a conversation about how travel impacts the planet and small things you can do to help.

Try to make these chats casual and curiosity-led. Kids this age can handle deeper discussions, and travel gives those topics context.

Cultural deep dives

You don't need to spend a fortune to give older kids a real taste of local culture. Sometimes, the cheapest experiences are the most memorable (and way more fun than another museum they'll sulk through).
- **Music exploration:** Tune into local music while you travel – on the radio, in cafés or even buskers on the street. Challenge your kids to find a new favourite song from that country.
- **Local legends and myths:** Forget boring dates and dusty facts – every place has its juicy stories. Ghosts, gods, tricksters, heroes

... dig into the tales that locals grew up with. They're often more gripping than Netflix and can be told over dinner or while wandering through the very streets where they "happened".
- **Festivals and rituals:** If you're lucky enough to visit during a local festival, you've struck gold. Get the kids involved in learning what's being celebrated, why it matters and what the traditions are. Food, costumes, dancing, fireworks – it's hands-on culture at its best. Even smaller rituals, like a weekly market or religious ceremony, can spark curiosity and great conversations.

The beauty of travel learning is that they don't even realise it's happening – no tests, no homework, just sneaky education disguised as adventure. When you travel, you realise just how *big* and beautiful the world is. Getting kids to notice those cultural quirks helps them become more open-minded, more empathetic and – let's be honest – way more interesting dinner guests in the future.

Global maths in real life

Leo absolutely loves maths, so any number-related game we make up on the road is an instant win. Even if your kid thinks maths is the root of all evil, it gets a major glow-up when it's tied to gelato, souvenirs or figuring out whether you've already missed the bus. Here are a few sneaky ways to turn the world into a maths classroom (without them realising):
- **Currency conversions:** Let them figure out what things cost in pounds. "This keyring is €5 – how much is that in *real* money?" Give them a daily budget in pounds and let them figure out what they can actually afford in the local currency.
- **Travel time challenges:** Get them working out journey times like mini train conductors. "If the train leaves at 14:07 and travels at 60mph for 40 minutes ..." (you get the idea). Throw in curveballs like delays, time zones or "we're stopping for chips" and, suddenly, it's real-world problem-solving with a side of chaos. (Just have your phone handy to work out the answers!)

- **Map scale maths:** Dust off a paper map (yes, the kind that doesn't tell you where Starbucks is) and have them plot your route. How far are you walking today? How long will it take given your pace (aka "snail speed with a buggy")? Add in hills, photo stops and essential café breaks if you want to keep things spicy.

You don't need worksheets – the world is one big maths lesson when you frame it right.

Foodie learning

Sampling food from around the world is hands down one of the best parts of travelling (and the main reason some of us book flights). With older kids, food becomes more than just fuel – it's an adventure, a story and a delicious way to learn. Try these ideas to get them just as excited:
- **International taste test:** Hit up a local shop or market and pick three new snacks or sweets to try together. Rate them as a family – flavour, texture, weirdness factor – and debate which one deserves the "holiday hall of fame". It's basically your own family version of *MasterChef*.
- **Cook a local dish:** Take a cooking class if you can, or just grab a recipe online and recreate it in your self-catering kitchen with local ingredients. Kids get to chop, stir and taste their way through a culture – and you all get dinner at the end. Win-win.
- **Restaurant role-play:** Hand over the reins at mealtimes. Let them order the food, ask for the bill and even work out the tip. It's surprisingly empowering, builds confidence and makes them feel properly grown-up.

Creative and expressive learning

Travel isn't just about ticking sights off a list – it's a goldmine for creativity. Pack a "creativity kit" (journal, sketchpad, glue stick, a few pens) and turn everyday travel moments into mini projects. Capturing a trip through words, doodles and photos helps kids notice more, process what they're seeing and bring home souvenirs you can't buy in a gift shop.

- **Travel journaling:** Forget the boring "Dear Diary" approach. Encourage them to jot down three cool things from each day, doodle a funny moment or stick in ticket stubs and receipts. The messier, the better – it's about making it theirs, not spelling every word right.
- **Photo challenges:** Set silly themes like "funny signs", "animals with attitude" or "the weirdest building we can find". Not only does it get them looking around instead of staring at their phone, but you'll also end up with some pretty epic family photo albums.
- **Street art and murals:** Encourage them to snap or sketch local graffiti, sculptures or murals. Chat about what it might mean or what it says about the place. Sometimes it's political, sometimes it's just a giant purple cat – either way, it sparks curiosity and conversation.

Geography meets adventure

Travel is geography you can actually touch, climb and sometimes get blisters from. Stairs become elevation practice, wind direction turns into a live compass lesson and even place names are little clues about the history and landscape. Here are a few ways to sneak some learning in while they're too busy adventuring to notice:

- **DIY scavenger hunts:** Make a list of geographical features to spot – cliffs, rivers, caves, mountains, palm trees, red soil, sand dunes; whatever's around. Give them a phone or camera and let them "collect" each one in photos. Extra points for the funniest captions.
- **Compass skills and orienteering:** Hand over a compass (yes, they still exist – you can even get them on your phone) or let them use a map app on a hike. Show them how to find north and track a route (Google how to do it yourself first, of course). It's part survival skill, part treasure hunt, and they'll love showing it off to friends later.
- **Track your trip:** Get them to plot your journey on a paper map or pin stops on a shared Google Map. Add fun facts, doodles or photos along the way. By the end, they've basically made their own personalised atlas – way cooler than anything they'll get in school.

SOCIAL MEDIA, PEER PRESSURE AND SCREENS

Travelling with older kids means you're not just packing sun cream and flip-flops – you're also likely bringing along TikTok, Snapchat and whatever social media app is trendy this week. Screens are part of their world, and pretending otherwise is like expecting a teenager to be chirpy at 7am. Probs not going to happen.

As a content creator, I see the positives in using these apps when they're approached responsibly – they can be creative tools, memory-makers and even brilliant travel guides. The trick isn't banning phones completely, but finding a balance that works for everyone. Here are some ideas:

Tips for tech balance

- **Set expectations early:** Have a chat before you go and make a family agreement about phone use. Nothing scary or military-grade – just simple boundaries like no phones at the dinner table or mornings tech-free until after breakfast. The golden rule? Everyone sticks to it, including you. (Yes, that means putting your own phone down too.)
- **Use phones creatively:** Encourage them to make a travel vlog, film a "day in the life" reel or keep a photo diary. They're still on their phones, but with purpose – and you'll end up with some hilarious, memory-packed content to look back on.
- **Let them take the lead on research:** Challenge them to find the best gelato in Rome or the coolest hidden beach in Greece – via Instagram or TikTok. They'll love being the family's "travel scout" and probably find places you wouldn't have.
- **Make screen-free moments meaningful:** It's much easier to ditch the phone when something awesome is happening. Plan activities where screens are impractical – hiking, wild swimming, rollercoasters, zip-lining – and the moment naturally takes over. No nagging required.
- **Agree to a rule of thumb for the whole family:** For example, screens are totally allowed, but only if they make the trip better.

Researching, creating, learning? Yes. Sitting in silence, ignoring each other in a Paris café while doomscrolling TikTok? Absolutely not.

Navigating social media pressures

Social media can be a brilliant way for kids to document and share their travels, but it also comes with pressure. Let's not pretend it's all sunshine and selfies. Social media can make even the best holiday feel like it's "not good enough". Teens (and, honestly, adults too) may worry about how they look in photos, whether they're posting the "right" thing or comparing their experience to someone else's highlight reel. Cue the anxiety spiral. It has happened to us all and will certainly happen to our kids. Here are a few things you can try to take the pressure off:

- **Start a conversation, not a lecture:** Have a real discussion about self-esteem, privacy and authenticity. Ask them how they *feel* when they're scrolling. Does it make them feel inspired or like they're missing out? Talk about filters, edits and the performative side of travel content. Keep it light, non-judgy and honest.
- **Discuss what's *not* posted:** Remind them that the "perfect" trip they saw online probably didn't include the mosquito bites, the missed train or the airport tantrum. Every trip has its bloopers – it's normal.
- **Encourage offline memories:** Some of the most magical moments are the ones we keep just for ourselves. A perfect sunset. A silly family joke. The best pizza ever. Let them know it's OK (even cool) to not post everything. Real connection > online reaction.

Apps that actually help

Not all screen time is doomscrolling. The right apps can make travel smoother, funnier and even sneakily educational:

- **Duolingo (or any language app):** Learning "hello" and "thank you" is good manners; being able to order a pizza in perfect Italian is basically a superpower. Turning it into a game keeps kids hooked.

PRIVACY, SAFETY AND BEING SMART ONLINE

Screens aren't going anywhere, so, instead of banning them, teach older kids how to use them wisely. A little digital street smart goes a long way when travelling.

- **Location tagging 101:** Posting "Here we are right now!" might feel fun, but it's safer to share *after* you've left a spot. Talk to them about why (hint: strangers knowing exactly where you are isn't ideal). Also check that any "share my location" settings are turned off unless it's with family.
- **Talk about who sees what:** Encourage them to keep personal accounts private or to be selective about what they share. It's a good reminder that once something's online, it's basically forever – and you can't always control who's watching.
- **Confidence over clout:** Teenagers love likes, but remind them that validation doesn't come from strangers double-tapping a selfie. Focus on being present in the moment – the gelato tastes just as good whether it gets 200 likes or none. Help them value memories over metrics.
- **Respectful sharing:** Chat about asking before posting pics of friends, family or locals. It's a lesson in kindness and consent, as much as digital safety.

- **Google Lens:** Point your phone at a menu, a sign or even a strange plant and it'll translate or identify it instantly. It's like having a pocket tour guide.
- **Spotify or Apple Music:** Let them curate the ultimate holiday playlist. By the end of the trip, every song will remind you of an adventure, a car ride or an inside joke. Bonus: it makes the school run back home feel way cooler when it's set to salsa, reggae or K-pop.
- **Video editing apps (such as CapCut and InShot):** Give them the green light to create travel vlogs, reels or photo montages. It's creativity over endless scrolling, and they'll end up with souvenirs they actually want to look back on.

Lead by example

The hard truth? If you're glued to your own phone, they'll follow suit. Try putting your phone away during meals, stop checking emails at the beach and model that it's OK to be *offline*. Your kids might roll their eyes, but they notice. And, deep down, they're grateful for it. I'm as bad as anyone for this, but I'm always trying to do better.

Remember: travelling together is a rare chance to really *connect* – not just with new places, but with each other. Help them make memories worth more than a like. Teach them that being present is powerful. And that no filter can top real joy.

This is a chance to teach digital mindfulness – without the lecture.

SIBLING DYNAMICS ON THE ROAD

If you're travelling with a mix of ages, keeping everyone happy can feel like a full-time job. But older kids can play a huge role in making things go smoothly – if you involve them in the right way:

- **Give them a bit of responsibility:** Even if it's something small like helping to pack snacks or working out how to get to the next spot.
- **Let them opt out of certain younger kid activities:** Let them choose something they'd rather do later on.

- **Build in moments just for them:** That might be a solo treat, a lie-in while the little ones go out or a later bedtime than the others.
- **Make sure they don't feel burdened:** It's natural to lean on older kids to help with younger siblings, but check they're genuinely OK with it. Helping out is fine; feeling like the stand-in parent is not.

Remind them that, while they don't need to be besties with their sibling(s) every second of the trip, their attitude really does set the tone. Travel has a sneaky way of building stronger sibling bonds – think late-night giggles in bunk beds, shared in-jokes and united "this is ridiculous" eye-rolls. Those moments are the glue that sticks.

Here's the thing: they might not thank you. They might grumble more than they smile. But they *will* remember. They'll remember the awful bunk bed that creaked like a haunted house. They'll remember the pizza in Naples that ruined all other pizzas. They'll remember the stranger who gave directions with hand gestures and a smile. They'll remember the inside jokes you shared on a rainy hike and when they slipped and got a muddy bum.

Even if they don't say it out loud, these moments stay with them. They shape the way they see the world – and how they see themselves in it.

Travelling with big kids is a unique window of opportunity – a time to bond, teach, explore and laugh together before life gets busier and more independent. By giving them a voice, encouraging responsibility and tailoring travel to their interests, you create something even more powerful than a holiday: shared memories and skills that will last a lifetime.

WHEN THINGS GO WRONG (BECAUSE SOMETIMES THEY WILL)

Flights get delayed. Museums are mysteriously closed. It rains for three days straight and the only entertainment left is counting ceiling tiles. With older kids, the challenge is keeping spirits up without the magic fix of stickers and a juice box. You can't sugar-coat reality, but you *can* show them how to roll with it.

Here are some ways to model resilience:
- **Be honest, but stay calm:** Share your own disappointment so they see it's normal to feel annoyed – then show them how to deal with it without spiralling.
- **Bring them into the problem-solving:** Ask them to help brainstorm alternatives. They might surprise you with ideas – and giving them a say makes them feel like part of the solution, not just passengers on the misery train.
- **Keep a "trip fails" list:** Write down or snap photos of the disasters as they happen. Later, they'll be the stories everyone laughs about: the hotel with no hot water, the meal that was *definitely* not what you ordered or the time Mum booked the wrong train. Travel fails often end up being the best family stories.

PRACTICAL TIPS FOR TRAVELLING WITH BIG KIDS

Packing tips
- Pack extra chargers, power banks and adapters – you'll need them!
- Bring a travel pillow, eye mask and headphones for everyone.
- Let them choose a small comfort item – a hoodie, snack stash or travel journal.

Managing sleep and jet lag
- Keep the first day slow and chilled – no "museum marathons" after a red-eye flight.
- Encourage them to stay awake until the local bedtime, even if they look like zombies. It pays off the next day.
- Don't over-schedule. They might look grown up, but they still need downtime (and naps aren't just for toddlers).

Food and eating out
- Let them choose where to eat sometimes – especially if you're somewhere unfamiliar.
- Encourage them to try new foods, but don't force it.
- Persuade them to order for themselves and work out the tip!

Giving them space

- If they're old enough (and sensible enough), let them stay back at the hotel or apartment while you do a younger-kid activity. A little independence goes a long way.
- Build in downtime so they're not constantly being dragged from one sight to the next. Sometimes doing nothing is exactly what everyone needs.
- If your accommodation has a teen club or hangout space, let them try it. Socialising with kids their own age is sometimes the real holiday highlight.

MY MOST-ASKED QUESTIONS
Here are quick answers to questions I'm asked most online, so you can skim and get on with your trip. For deeper dives, see the chapters noted.

Pregnancy FAQs
Q: When's the best time to travel in pregnancy?
A: Usually the second trimester (weeks 13–27): you will likely have more energy, fewer symptoms and your bump still isn't too big. *(See "The best time to travel during pregnancy", p177.)*

Q: Do I need a doctor's letter to fly?
A: You will likely need a doctor's letter to fly from 28 weeks; policies vary by airline and route. Check before you book and carry proof of dates. Screenshot the policy. *(See "Safe flying while pregnant", p181.)*

Q: What should I look for in travel insurance?
A: Pregnancy isn't typically classed as a condition, but you should declare any pregnancy complications. Check maternity care coverage and cancellation terms. Make sure there is adequate medical coverage and that all the activities you plan to do are covered in the policy. *(See p179.)*

Q: How do I handle nausea on travel days?
A: Small, frequent snacks; ginger/mints; sickness bands; aisle seats; avoid strong smells; pack a sick bag and your go-to meds (OK'd by your midwife). *(See "Managing pregnancy symptoms on the road", p188.)*

Baby and toddler FAQs
Q: Are under-twos free on planes?
A: Not usually "free" – they fly as lap infants for a small fee/taxes, or you can pay for a seat and use an approved car seat. *(See p200.)*

Q: Can I bring formula, breast milk or baby food through security?
A: Yes, in reasonable quantities – even over 100ml – subject to screening. Pack it where you can easily access it.

Q: How do I sterilise on the go?
A: Cold-water sterilising tablets are our go-to as you can use them anywhere. Microwave sterilisation bags are useful to sterilise and then store the items clean before using (just make sure you have a microwave). Boiling works in self-catering kitchens.

Q: Can I take our car seat abroad?
A: Yes, most airlines allow you to check in a pram and car seat for free. Check ahead – a few budget airlines may only allow one item. *(See p200.)*

Q: Do you have any tips to deal with ears popping on flights?
A: Feed during take-off/landing (from bottle/breast/cup), try a dummy and avoid flying if your kid has a heavy cold if you can help it. *(See p202.)*

Big kid and teen FAQs

Q: How do we balance screen time on holiday?
A: Agree boundaries before you go (such as no phones at meals), then channel usage into vlogs, photo diaries or research missions. *(See p238.)*

Q: How do I get them involved without surrendering the trip?
A: Offer parent-approved choices: then they can vote on activities or hotels. Assign real tasks (tickets, directions) and give a daily snack/souvenir budget. *(See "Get them involved", p229.)*

Q: Are there any quick ways to make city breaks land with older kids?
A: Mix one "wow" sight with one hands-on activity and one food stop. Add a photo challenge or interactive tour/VR to avoid museum fatigue. *(See "Learning on the road", p232.)*

Q: What helps with motion sickness in bigger kids?
A: Front seats on coaches/cars often cause less motion sickness. Get them to focus on the horizon rather than staring out of the side of the vehicle. Light snacks, frequent air and avoiding reading/screens while in motion can all help. Take pre-approved meds if needed.

Final Thoughts:
JUST START

The trip ends, the washing machine starts on a seemingly endless cycle and life rushes back in. There's sand in the buggy and new in-jokes at the dinner table. You made it – and you made lifelong family memories in the process.

Life doesn't follow a neat itinerary. There are layovers and delays. Highs that take your breath away and lows that make you question if you'll ever feel joy again. I've lived them: the spontaneous baby, the heartbreaking losses, the scary births, the full-blown tantrums at airport gates. But through it all, there's been one constant: the power of travel to reconnect, reset and remind me of who I am – and who we are as a family.

I've written this book not just as a guide to finding cheap flights and packing light, but as a reminder that *you can do this*. You *deserve* to do this. Whatever your story – whether you're bouncing back from heartbreak, navigating toddler chaos, solo parenting or just desperately in need of a nap – travel has a way of meeting you where you are.

It doesn't have to be far-flung or fancy. Sometimes it's a cheap city break. Sometimes it's a last-minute camping trip. Sometimes it's just stepping out of the day to day to remember that life is more than laundry and lunchboxes.

You don't have to have it all figured out. You just have to start.

Say yes to the trip. Say yes to the ice cream before lunch. Say yes to being the parent who tries, even if it's messy and loud and not Instagram-perfect.

Because the world is out there – and your family belongs in it.

Not someday. Not when it's easier.

Now.

WITH THANKS

This book exists because so many people believed in the idea that family travel doesn't have to be impossible, miserable or ridiculously expensive – it can be joyful, messy, affordable and real. Thank you for believing in me when I wasn't so sure myself, and for giving me your time when mine ran out.

To my family: to my husband, João, for shouldering the late bedtimes, early wake-ups and "just one more paragraph" weekends; you have always believed in me and given me the confidence to do this. To my parents, who have always stepped in with childcare, meals and support: you gave me hours I couldn't have found alone. And to my boys: wherever we are, if we're together, it's an adventure. This one's for you.

To my team: Thank you Sam, my agent, for championing this book from the very first messy pitch I made; Jo and Zoë, for believing in the concept from day one; and Julia, for shaping my ramble into something readable and beautiful.

To my community: The 700,000+ of you across Instagram and TikTok, newsletter readers and website visitors – your DMs, comments and emails have built this book. Thank you for trusting me with your trips and joining me on this journey.

Lastly, to anyone walking a harder road to family – through loss, IVF, fear or fatigue – I see you. If this book gives you a little permission to say yes to joy, then every late night was worth it.

Index

A
Abu Dhabi 99, 104
accommodation 30–31, 57–73
   accessibility 31, 66, 67
   all-inclusive deals 61, 62–3
   best deals 70–73
   breakfasts 60
   choosing a destination 93
   city breaks 102
   creative options 68–70
   DIY booking 42
   entertainment in hotels 27
   food costs 23–5
   hidden costs 22, 72
   for little kids 212, 215, 217
   package deals 40–41
   in pregnancy 186
   rentals 69
   road trips 110
   roadside hotels 127–9
   safety 66
   self-catering 61–2, 63
   sleeping arrangements 30, 64–5
   staycations 127–9
   sustainable travel 164
   theme parks 135
   travelling with babies 198–9
adventure travel 231
AI, DIY booking 43
air conditioning 157, 186
air travel *see* flights
Airbnb 69
airport transfers 25–6, 50–51
Albania 45, 94, 99
alcohol 158
Algarve 9, 93, 98, 162
all-inclusive holidays 61, 62–3
amenities, self-catering 65–6
Amsterdam 104
apartments 21, 30, 64, 69
Apple Music 241
apps 239–41
ATM fees 29, 30
ATOL/ABTA protection 41
audiobooks 117, 185, 216, 232
Austria 52–3, 113
Azores 95, 104

B
B&Bs 70
babies 191–207
   camping 153
   equipment 66
   flights 21, 195, 199–200, 246–7
   hidden costs 22, 48
   planning first trips 196–205
balconies, safety 66
banks, hidden costs 29–30
Barcelona 98, 104, 162, 231
bassinets 200, 202
beach holidays 26, 44–5, 214–15, 231
big kids 225–45
   benefits of travel 227–9
   involving 229–30, 247
   learning on the road 232–7
   sibling dynamics 241
   social media, peer pressure and screens 238–41, 247
   types of holiday 230–31
   when things go wrong 243
birth certificates, babies 196
blackout curtains 66, 199
boarding passes 47
boats
   cruises 52, 180, 204
   ferries 51, 52, 178–9
   narrowboats 70
Bosnia and Herzegovina 94, 104
bottle-feeding 203–4, 246–7
breakdown cover 115
breakfasts 23–5, 60
budgets 19–35
   big kids 229–30, 235
   camping 144
   exchange rates 29, 93, 229, 235
   hidden costs 22–31
   holiday parks 156–9
   road trips 114–15
   saving for holiday 31–3
   staycations 127
   sustainable travel 164
   Whoops Fund 32
Bulgaria 94–5, 99
buses 25, 50, 130

C
cabins 70
camper vans 111–12, 118–19
camping 69–70, 111, 114, 118–19, 127, 128, 132, 141–63
Canada 160
Canary Islands 97, 101
cancellation policies 71, 72–3
Cape Verde 101

cars
  car seats 115, 200, 202–3, 247
  hiring 26, 50, 111, 115, 202–3
  parking 60, 67
  road trips 51, 52, 107–21, 188–9
check-in, flights 21, 46–7, 200, 207
city breaks 45–6, 102–3, 230–31, 247
clothes 48, 149, 153, 180, 184, 218
coaches 51, 52
cots 22, 59, 64, 66, 153, 199
Covid-19 pandemic 81–6
creativity 219–20, 236–7
credit cards 29–30
Croatia 45, 99, 104, 119, 160
cruises 28, 52, 180, 204
culture 218–19, 233–4
cycling 52–3
Cyprus 81, 98, 101
Czech Republic 101

D

destinations 91–105
  choosing 92–3
  hidden gems 94–6
  for little kids 212–13
  sustainable travel 164
  travelling with babies 197–8
  weekend and city breaks 102–3
  when to travel 96–102
discounts 27, 31, 51, 70–1, 93, 134
dishwashers 66
DIY booking 41–9
Dominican Republic 105
Dubai 98, 104
Duolingo 239

E

ears, popping on flights 202, 216, 247
Egypt 97
emergencies 67, 151
England 119
entertainment
  camping 144, 147
  hidden costs 26–7
  holiday parks 155, 157–8
  in-flight 216
  road trips 117
  staycations 129–32
  theme parks 26, 103, 130, 134–9
equipment
  babies 66
  camping 144–6, 151–2

eSIMs 29
Estonia 113
etiquette 234
Europe, destinations 94–5
exchange rates 29, 93, 229, 235

F

family bonding 227
fatigue, in pregnancy 188–9
festivals 235
Finland 113
fire safety 67
first aid kits 149–51, 184, 203
flexibility, road trips 116–17
flights 37–50
  babies 21, 195, 199–200, 246–7
  booking 21, 41–9
  choosing a destination 93
  hidden costs 46–9
  layovers 45–6, 55
  little kids 195, 214–16
  luggage 21
  neurodiverse families 54–5
  package deals 40–41
  pregnancy and 178, 180, 181–3, 186, 246
  sustainable travel 165
Florida 100, 206
food
  all-inclusive holidays 62–3
  big kids 236, 244
  camping 152–3
  choosing a destination 92
  city breaks 102
  hidden costs 22–5
  holiday parks 157, 158
  picky eaters 222–3
  in pregnancy 180, 186, 189
  road trips 114–15
  self-catering 61–3, 74–5
  staycations 132
  theme parks 135–6
food poisoning 183
France 51, 52–3, 94, 105, 113, 119, 160–61, 197

G

The Gambia 101
games 117
garden camping 145
geocaching 103, 130–31
geography 237
Georgia 96, 104
Germany 98, 119

Google Lens 241
Greece 95, 98, 105, 160

H
healthcare 67, 82–7, 180, 186, 198
heartburn, in pregnancy 186, 189
hidden costs 22–31
high chairs 66, 153
hiking trails 26
history, learning about 219, 232–3
holiday parks 52, 69–70, 144, 154–9
home, staycations 128
hospitals 67
hostels 68–9
hotels see accommodation
house-sitting 68, 126, 127
Hungary 99

I
Iceland 104, 113
independence, big kids 228, 231, 245
Indonesia 104
insurance 28, 47, 115, 178, 179, 198, 246
internet 28–9, 144
interrailing 51
Italy 95, 100, 104, 105, 119, 161

J
Japan 46, 64, 105, 119, 161
jetlag 220, 244
Jobs, Steve 10
journaling 237

K
kitchens 65, 199

L
languages 218–19, 233–5, 239–40
Lapland 98, 118, 119
Latvia 113
laundry 49, 217
layovers, flights 45–6, 55
Les Castels 161
LGBTQ+ families 31
libraries 27, 130
Lithuania 113
little kids 209–23
    accommodation 212
    destinations 212–13
    flights 214–16, 246
    learning on the road 218–20
    packing for 213, 217–18
    picky eaters 222–3
    preparing for trip 213

little kids (cont.)
    when to travel 214–15
Lombok 104
loyalty schemes 71, 158
luggage see packing
lunches 23, 62

M
Madeira 98
Malaysia 95
Maldives 105
Malta 100
markets 27
maternity leave 195
maths 235–6
medical care 67, 82–7, 180, 186, 198
medications 179, 184
microwaves 65
mini cruises 52
mobility issues 31
money see budgets
Montenegro 95, 99
Morocco 101
motion sickness 247
movies 130
museums 27, 66, 102, 103, 131, 219
music 118, 241

N
nappies 153, 197, 206
narrowboats 70
nature 131, 144, 218, 233
nausea 179–80, 183, 188, 246
Netherlands 51, 104, 162
neurodiverse families 31, 54–5, 136
New Zealand 162
NHS 82–7
nightlights 217
Norway 104, 113, 163

O
obstacle courses 131
off-season travel 93, 96–7

P
package holidays 30, 33, 40–41, 73
packing
    big kids 229, 244
    camping 148–54
    flights 21, 46–7
    insurance 28
    for little kids 213, 217–18
    packing cubes 49, 217
    packing light 48–9

packing (cont.)
    and pregnancy 183–5
    road trips 120–21
    sustainable travel 165
    travelling with babies 201
Paris 25, 27, 105
parking 60, 67
parks 26, 102, 103
passes 93, 134, 135, 163
passports, babies 196
phones 28–9, 238–41, 247
photos 131–2, 187, 195, 205, 237
planning checklist 76–7
playgrounds 27, 92, 103
Poland 97, 99
Portugal 45, 95, 98, 105, 113, 119, 162
prams 21, 48, 67, 198, 200
pregnancy 170–73, 177–89
    flights 246
    road trips 188–9
    safety 179–83
    spa treatments 182
    what to pack 183–5
    when to travel 177–9, 246
privacy, online 240
public transport 25, 50, 93, 165, 203

R
rainy days 66
restaurants 23–5, 217, 244
road trips 107–21, 197
roaming charges 28–9
Rome 87, 98
routes, planning 116

S
safety
    accommodation 66
    cruises 204
    little kids 217
    online 240
    pregnancy 179–83
    road trips 115
    travelling with babies 199
St. Lucia 105
school holidays 71, 98, 100, 156, 214
schools, fines 214
Scotland 112, 125
screen shots 47, 151
screens 66, 229, 238–41, 247
security, airport 55, 183, 206–7
self-catering holidays 23, 61–2, 63, 65–6, 74–5, 157
Seville 98

Seychelles 105
shoes 49, 181, 184
shoulder seasons 100, 156, 165
showers 67, 147
sibling dynamics 241
Sicily 87, 99
single parents 31, 197
sleep, babies 203, 204
Slovenia 94, 99, 105
slow travel 231
snacks 47, 63, 152–3, 216, 222
social media 238–41
socks, compression 181, 184, 189
South Africa 95
spa treatments 182
Spain 45, 94, 99, 104, 113, 119, 162–3
spas 159, 178, 182, 187
Spotify 241
Sri Lanka 95, 101
staycations 96, 123–33, 179
storytelling 117, 232
supermarkets 23, 135
sustainable travel 164–5
Sweden 113, 163
swimming pools 27, 66, 130, 186, 204
Switzerland 105

T
Taiwan 95–6, 105
tantrums 221
taxes, tourist 22, 72
taxis 25, 50
Tenerife 101
Thailand 101
theme parks 26, 103, 130, 134–9
tipping 27
toddlers *see* little kids
toilets 112, 147, 215
tolls, road 114
torches 146, 149
tourist taxes 22, 72
traditions, staycations 131–3
trains 25, 50, 51, 93, 114, 130, 178–9
transaction fees 29
travel 37–53
    alternatives to flying 51–3
    choosing a destination 92, 93
    hidden costs 25–6
    pregnancy and 177–184
    sustainable travel 165
travel insurance 28, 47, 115, 178, 179, 198, 246
The Travel Mum 40, 42, 45, 55, 86–7, 170

treasure hunts 128, 129–31
treehouses 70
Turkey 99

U
university dorms 129
Uruguay 96
USA 100, 163, 206

V
vaccinations, babies 196
Valencia 104, 162
Venice 94, 103, 105
video editing apps 241
villas 30, 64
visas 206

W
walking tours 26–7
washing machines 65
water, drinking 47, 183, 184
water parks 26, 131, 137
websites, comparison 28, 42, 47, 71–2, 92
weekend breaks 102–3
Whoops Fund 32
Wi-Fi 29, 66, 72, 128, 144, 155, 228
wild camping 111, 114
windows, safety 66
wine 23
wristbands, safety 137, 217

Z
Zanzibar 105
Zika virus 179, 186
zoos 27, 103, 215, 218